THE PLANETARY MIND

THE PLANETARY MIND

Becoming Fully Human in the 21st Century

MICHAEL W. SIMPSON, PH.D.

Blue Dolphin Publishing

Published in association with Bluefox Productions
by Blue Dolphin Publishing, Inc.
P.O. Box 8, Nevada City, CA 95959
Orders: 1-800-643-0765
Web: www.bluedolphinpublishing.com

ISBN: 1-57733-130-3

Library of Congress Cataloging-in-Publication Data

Simpson, Michael W.
    The planetary mind : becoming fully human in the 21st century / Michael
W. Simpson.
        p. cm.
    Includes bibliographical references and index.
    ISBN 1-57733-130-3 (alk. paper)
    1. New Thought. I. Title.

BF639.S615 2004
299'.93—dc22

                                                                2004013804

Printed in the United States of America

5   4   3   2   1

Table of Contents

INTRODUCTION

Global Identity Crisis

IN PSYCHOTHERAPY a patient breaks down and cries out to his therapist "... please tell me who I am!" That night, the psychologist, in a conversation with her casual lover, breaks into tears when he refers to her syncretized system of beliefs, composed as it is of equal parts Christian orthodoxy, medieval monasticism, and "new age" Eastern mysticism, as "backwards superstition." That same lover, after he stalks out disappointed that such a brilliant doctor and healer could be so wrapped up in her past life regressions, reincarnated ascended masters, and space ship commanders, goes alone to his apartment and enters into a state of deep contemplative meditation where he prays, as a poet, to the lost gods of the ancient oracles seeking his eternal name in the mists of antiquated epochs. Knowing who we are can be difficult.

To what do we owe our deeply felt crisis of identity? There is no one cause. What we feel within is but a reflection of what is occurring around us. Identity has been based for eons upon a set of complex relationships between the individual and the environment embodied in culture and language, which are the great mediators between them. But these mediators are eroded beneath the tread of modern society and communication.

Sioux writer Elizabeth Cook-Lynn noted that the singular defining characteristic of modern American people is the collective search for an answer to the question "who am I?" The singular defining characteristic of indigenous peoples is the maintenance of the understanding of "who we are." Individualism and democracy have resulted in many material

1

and political advances, but have led, at the same time, to alienation, fragmentation, divisiveness, selfishness, greed, and the growing planetary identity crisis.

The prevalence and popularity of self-help books, channelers, crystal healers, empowerment workshops, multi-cultural gurus, and fundamentalist, evangelical television preachers are all expressions of this problem. We live in a world which has never before existed. We wildly seek for some new model, an altered paradigm, a revised world view which allows us to connect ourselves to a greater whole without losing our sense of individual value and worth. There is an obvious need for a new approach to living and dying in the twenty-first century.

We seek understanding of the changes enfolding us but are at the same time frightened by the implications. Some return to the past, some hedonistically hold to the moment, and a few brave souls look cautiously into the future hoping to glimpse something that will save them from massive confusion. The world is changing ever more rapidly. Conflicts and tensions prevail around the globe. Some populations live in the extremes of deprivation that hearken back to the middle ages, while only a few hours flight-time away others build palaces and live in resplendent luxury and die from the diseases of over-consumption. How are we to deal with the contrasts?

We can ignore them and retreat into cocoons of indifference. We can become fanatics and join the countless causes that seek, based on the old world view which no longer suffices, to clearly redefine the human experience. We can engage in the use of psychotropic agents as the shaman of our ancestral tribes did when environmental pressures got to the point someone needed to alter their frame of reference in order to see alternatives. Or, we can simply give it as little thought as possible and indifferently live from day to day. Is there no hope? Is there an alternative?

It is possible that a view of our lives and the world we live in can be synthesized which will allow us to come to terms with our time and place. We can learn to "believe" in a way which transforms our conscious awareness and at once ties us into the greater wholeness of being of which we are each tiny, but significant parts, and brings us a feeling of quietude within ourselves. This in turn can inspire others to likewise seek out the source of what makes one feel whole and able to calmly participate in the process of transformation and the accompanying turmoil which inevitably goes with it. The resulting optimism, the feeling that the world makes sense, that things are somehow connected, that we know who we are, can bring us to rest, and put an end to the crisis.

The crisis is over when alienation, fragmentation, and the breakdown in the integrity of the identity are overcome and we are joined, brought together, and reunited at their core, within the greater whole. The confusing world we live in, especially in the developed, post-industrial, information-age nation-states of the twenty-first century— which profess values, beliefs, and attitudes, and act in ways based upon outmoded and archaic, religious, racial, nationalist and moral codes— cannot long continue to exist as it is.

We must not underestimate or discount the value of the beliefs that have brought us to this terminal point. We see what we believe. The world that appears to our senses is but a partial view hemmed in by the limits of our faculties. And culture has perpetually attempted to formulate and institutionalize a set of ideas, metaphors, and analogies which describe both the limits of perception, and the limitless nature of what lies beyond both sense and belief. The meaning of our lives is embodied in the languages with which we describe and define our experience.

On occasion a set of ideas is created which, by analogy, is similar to a new virus. Whether the ideas are those of animism, religion, science, or whatever, they find the mental environment of whole populations receptive to them and proliferate. They infuse the minds of the hosts with signals that alter their language and thus their perceptions, and the world of those who embrace them.

In our time and place, out of the confusion and conflicts being generated by the systemic transformation we are undergoing on a planetary scale, I have found only one seed of thought which appears to be sufficient for the purpose of redefining the process we are all part of. *This is the model of interconnected systems joining together as extensions of the universal mind to form a global entity.* This entity is able to organize and regulate its own energy systems and resources in an efficient, equitable fashion. Thus it insures at least minimal subsistence for all, and a subsequent lessening of conflict throughout the world. But adopting such a view means a full transformation of our personal perceptions, our families and societies, of our nations and races.

The way in which a personality overcomes the crisis of transformation and approaches an integrated state of being and a coherent identity
is through an alteration of the basic premises upon which the old identity
was built. When the old identity disintegrates, by a sort of critical mass
fission, it must have enough strength in its core to reform at a new level
of order and complexity, through the complementary process of fusion.

This requires one to reflect and sort through those elements of their
system, to determine which are to be most useful and valuable in terms
of contributing to reformation, and dispensing with all others. Thus the
language which one uses changes, and this alters perceptions, objects of
perceptions, and relationships between all systemic elements. Out of the
confusion new premises are formed and the core of the being, which is
life seeking to continue living and growing, reforms. The internal being
reorganizes its boundary layers to create the expression of a new identity.

In systemic terms this process is the same for a molecule, a cell, an
injured organ, a confused individual identity, a tension-ridden disintegrating culture, or a planet. By analogy the process can be extended in
every direction. By adopting an altered frame of reference based on the
perceptions and sense of identity of an integrated, whole mind, the
identity crisis can be overcome and the psyche healed with time and hard
work.

The following chapters describe the foundations of an altered paradigm called "Hologenics," a way of viewing human experience so as to
generate an integrated, interconnected awareness: a planetary mind. It
tells the individual "I" how to look at the world in such a way as to see
beyond the divisions and confusions inherent in an apparently fragmented world, and to find the true self, to see that "we" are unified within
the universal mind.

I

The Voice Within

HAVE YOU EVER WONDERED how you talk to yourself inside your head, or considered just what that "little voice" is? You see, there's a problem here, because you simply can't have a "voice" within. There is no air in your skull to vibrate, so there is no sound. There are no vocal chords or tongue to speak with, and no ears to hear with in the mysterious depths of your brain.

According to psychologists the ability to engage in "self-talk" is one of the primary attributes of individual awareness. By "talking" to ourselves internally we are better able to reflect upon, monitor, organize, and regulate our activities. Without the voice within we would, in effect, be rather mindless. Spoken and written language, the external forms of self-talk, would not exist as we know them, and civilization might never have begun.

The voice within actually seems to be a side effect of the activity of what Dr. Carl Pribram, of Stanford University, describes as "helical, closed-loop, feedback circuits," which are found throughout the brain, including the sound and word processing systems.

According to Dr. Pribram's "TOTE" model of the operation of these circuits, incoming sounds and words are Tested, Organized, Tested, and then Exit the system. During the second test the original signal is "fed back" to a previous area, where it is compared to memories, sampled for response value, then fed forward to an associated area, such as the pre-motor area previous to being transformed into an outgoing signal: speech.

Sounds, in the form of pressure waves, enter the ear from the air as vibrations that are passed, via the eardrum, into the bony formations of the inner ear, and into the fluid medium of the cochlea where they are passed to the brain stem and transformed into electrochemical codes. The primary audio area receives the coded signals, riding the carrier waves that represent sounds. Those signals representing words are fed forward and recognized in Werneke's area, which is located in the left temporal lobe of the brain, not too far from the ear. Once there, the signals are routed along many channels and tested in relation to memory, and then sent to Broca's area where they are scanned for order, meaning, and where an appropriate response is generated. The signals then move to the pre-motor area where they undergo their last test and are sent to the motor area where the signals that stimulate the lungs, muscles, larynx, tongue, lips, and other principles of speech originate and exit the system as our physical voice.

But the signal, during this last test, must be compared to previous patterns of response. It seems that these electrochemical vibratory patterns must be fed back into anterior audio areas where they are perceived as if they were any other incoming signal. We then perceive, or "hear" the voice within. This feedback process is a sort of self-correction system which allows us to screen, or test what we are about to say before we say it, giving us time to think before we speak and, if necessary, change the response we are about to make before it can turn into spoken, audible words.

So, the next time you hear the voice within, remember that it's not really a voice at all, but the brain communicating with itself, and that, without it, we would not be aware of ourselves as we are. The voice within is thus one basis for self-awareness and internal communications.

If we extrapolate this type of systemic process to the planetary level of human experience, we begin to see some very interesting possibilities? Is it possible that the identity of the planet is developing towards some sort of self-awareness as it communicates with itself through the telecommunications networks? Is there any reason for hope regarding our being able to find a means of overcoming the global identity crisis, given this possibility? Let us continue our exploration.

Dream Seeing

"Who is watching your dreams?" a Zen koan asks. As a corollary to the voice within it can be said that we also have an "image" within. Sometimes this is called insight. But, as with the voice, there is a slight problem, one which psychologists and Zen masters alike have been aware of and thus compelled to wrestle with for a long time. And that is the fact that there is no light in the brain, no eyes to see with, no specific generator of the imagery or internal envisioning capacity of our imagination and dreams.

What eyes are we using? Why is it that perceptive individuals from ancient monks to modern doctors have all agreed that the brain cannot tell the difference between an integrated, internally generated image and a visual phenomenon coming through the eyes? Maxwell Maltz, in his classic book, *Psychocybernetics,* says that whatever we visualize as complete will be brought into manifest reality over time. The internal motivations, conceptions, and words needed to bring this about will come into being simply by our seeing the whole. Any artist or child knows that the way to make what you want is to visualize it completely, and only then concern yourself with the details of materials, appropriate processes, and effective methods.

Ancient Celtic bards were called "illusion casters" by their people, and had the power to convey to their audience, through audio, visual, and tactile means, a sense of being present in the middle of whatever was being described. Whether the eyes of the watchers were open or closed didn't matter to the most proficient bards. And remember, Homer was said to be blind, yet he created great works with exciting imagery and his recitations entertained many. Visualization is as old as humanity. But who, or what, is doing the watching?

It has been found that the pineal gland, a cone-shaped structure in the middle of the brain, secretes a chemical related to one of nature's most powerful hallucinogens: harmine. This chemical is called by the name 6-methoxytetrahydroharman. The effects of harmine intoxication include the ability to transpose fantasy upon reality in such a way that they seem to be the same. There are bright flashes of light in the peripheral vision, a dreamy drowsiness, and even reports of sensations of flight, communications with extraterrestrial entities, and telepathic experiences.

Neurologists have found that the pineal gland is indirectly connected to the occipital lobes, the centers of vision, through the sub-thalamic nuclei, and thus might have some functional relationship to visual experience—and visionary experience as well. What all of this suggests is that there is, perhaps in the pineal center, a possible source of the watcher, or viewer of the internal visualizations of imaginations and dreams.

And through the process of entrainment, the brain synchronizes its own activities with those of what is perceived. This allows us to give it a name, an explanation for the profound experiences we have when we watch a movie, see our favorite lover, or have a visionary experience. We are transported into a realm of awareness where all things are whole. The greater unity is apparent, rather than merely suggested, as it is by our daily experiences. This mode of vision does not rely upon the eyes.

This power of "dream seeing" or visualization is a key to creativity and self-awareness. Through it we can create whatever we imagine or dream. It is the watcher within, the pineal, "third eye," interpreter of patterns and fields of color, looking out into the constellations of activity in the sky of the mind, that sees what is beyond mere eyesight. If our brains are microcosms of the universe, receivers of signals which are patterns of energy in formations that give meaning to our experience and shape to our world—for it has been known since our earliest beginnings that what cannot be named does not exist for us—then what we see within are the potentials that, when projected onto material substance, or into the actions which make up our lives, are expressions of the universal mind of creation in action.

It is said that among some New World tribes the first Europeans walked without being seen—until a shaman saw them and recognized them as spirit beings come to fulfill ancient prophecies. Only then did they become visible to the people in general. The power of seeing, being such as it is, has always fascinated those who study *how* we see rather than *what*. It has become common knowledge among them that what we see is only a part of what is actually there in space-time's incalculable dimensions, the spirit world of our prehistoric ancestors, the mind in creation. And yet, by seeing the inherent patterns around us and giving them form within, we create in ourselves not only the seen, but the unseen elements of our world as well. By giving our visions form in names, materials, or other sorts of storage mediums we project patterns representative of the mysterious, magical, numinous power that is at the root of the process of creation within us, and throughout the universe.

Through responsible use of this power we shape ourselves, our surroundings, and the world. And the planet, by using this same power, is imagining us! Thus it might be said that it is through human activity that the earth gained the ability to look at itself. The image of the earth as seen from the moon is unique in the life of the living world. The planet has existed for more than four billion years, and never had a mirror. It is through human eyes that the Earth first saw itself as a whole. We thus share in the creative power of the universe and the planet that is our home. By seeing what we are we increase our ability to use our capacities and improve our lot. But misuse and faulty conceptions of the reflective power often lead to disastrous results. So let us consider how we might create within ourselves a global vision and a sane world within the universal mind.

Einstein's Brain

The brain of one of our greatest scientists is sitting in a jar of formaldehyde on a shelf above a water cooler in a laboratory in Weston, Missouri. This powerful thinker willed his brain to posterity for the sake of the sciences he loved. Any researcher can order up a cubic centimeter of Einstein's brain for purposes of laboratory study.

Dr. Marian Diamond, a well-known authority on the effects of enriched environments upon the growth and development of the brain, determined, in her studies with rats, that a richer environment leads to significant increases in brain weight, glial cell inter-connectivity, and information processing potentials. She theorized that what is true for rats might be true for humans as well. So, she decided to obtain a bit of Einstein's brain, from the areas known to deal with mathematics and other higher abstract functions, and test her hypothesis.

Her studies verified the theory. She sliced the great man's brain and upon viewing found that it had a much higher percentage of connections between neurons than a normal brain in the areas associated with mathematical ability. Albert was generally more intelligent than most people, and I wondered if his higher intelligence could in fact be a result of more connections.

I called Dr. Diamond at her lab and asked her if higher intelligence could be said to be related to higher levels of inter-connectivity. She said, simply, "yes," then went on to describe why she thought this to be true, and how, since Einstein could also play classical violin, he probably had higher levels of inter-connectivity in his musical processing systems as well.

Dr. Diamond's experiments with Einstein's brain suggest that the more varied our interactions within ourselves, with others, and with the environment, the greater the increase in connectivity which results. The better connected we are, the more we can see and get done. The way we frame our reality shapes our experience and development. The broader our frame of reference, the more connections we make, and the less we thus feel limited by common boundaries. The more intelligent and aware we become, the better we are able to organize and regulate our lives.

There are many areas and systems of signal processing in our brains—a partial list might include verbal, musical, visual, numerical, associative, and kinesthetic—and all are connected to one another directly or indirectly. There is a direct connection between the audio and visual systems called the arcuate fasciculus. Another structure called the angular gyrus also plays a part. The better connected such areas are within themselves, and with one another, the greater the thinking power of the individual.

There are, of course, other factors, besides glial interconnectivity, which contribute to higher intelligence and expanded awareness, such as brain weight and size, and the amount of fuel delivered in the form of glucose/oxygen. Additionally, external factors such as the richness of the early environment, and subsequent training and education in the use of one's abilities also play a part.

Still, there is but a thin line between high excitement and over-stimulation, and this threshold varies from one person to the next. What leads to more interconnections for one might lead to psychosis for another. Thresholds vary; yet, in any case, an enriched environment during development, if properly composed, can lead to higher intelligence and greater awareness.

A living being needs to be as aware as possible of its inner states, and the state of the external environment in relation to itself, in order to reach full development of its potential for organizing and regulating the interconnected systems of its makeup. We use our brains and move to interact with and affect the environment, and the environment we create for ourselves, in turn, affects and alters our brains, bodies, and lives. The effects of this sort of dynamic interaction cannot be underestimated.

In the global system it is evident that the degree of complexity and amount of interconnection between parts is increasing in direct proportion to increases in population and technological developments. The environment is becoming ever more enriched, the elements are becoming ever more interconnected, as are we humans. This is what Einstein's brain has to tell us. These internal and environmental developments are the foundation upon which an expanded view of ourselves can be built.

At the neuronal level more connections result from enrichment, likewise at the personal, social, and planetary levels. What does this say about our developing consciousness of who we are? Let's consider its evolution.

The Living Planet

Just how is it that the planet Earth has come to be covered with the limitless diversity of living forms we know of—not to mention the ones we don't know about, or can't be aware of? We live in what amounts to a rarefied misty atmosphere a few miles thick that, by analogy, is much like a Polaroid photograph. As we spin around the sun, organized atomic, molecular, and chemical patterns develop as the photoelectric effect causes electrons to be kicked loose, due to Brownian motion. Light and energy are released in the process, as matter precipitates out of the elemental organic soup into the wondrous forms of nature. We are part of a process of planetary photo development. The light of the sun interacts with the earth's delicate membrane, this blue envelope, and over the ages the world we live in has developed as a result of these processes which our arts, religions, and sciences have tried to comprehend, express and explain for eons.

According to the research of Dr. Margulis, of Boston University, and Dr. Lovelock in England, originators of the "Gaia Theory," the earth is a living planet. It fulfills the basic criteria used to define a living system. It "metabolizes" in that it gathers, stores, and uses energy in a transformational process that becomes ever more orderly, complex, and efficient. It "grows" through reproductive processes of various sorts and adapts to changes through the resulting diversity of life it brings about. It is self-organizing, and self-regulating in that it is an integrated system. Through processes we are only just beginning to understand and express as laws which describe causes and effects, it develops in a way which acts to preserve its integrity, stability, and coherence. It achieves homeostasis, dynamic equilibrium. It could even "reproduce"—but we'll return to that possibility later.

As Dr. Lewis Thomas suggested in *The Lives of a Cell*, the planet acts like a vast cell: diverse, complex, and cooperative, where all the parts combine to form an interconnected whole that is greater than the sum of the parts. So, if the planet is indeed alive, how does it maintain itself and stay that way?

The planet must, by analogy, have some sort of "brain," and, as a result of this process of directed intelligence, be developing a "mind" of its own. It is developing a form of consciousness which supersedes and dwarfs our human awareness by many orders of systemic magnitude. In order for a living system to maintain itself it must be aware of itself, and as a result be able to organize and regulate its own activities through feedback processes in such a way as to maintain a dynamic steady state. Thus it is able to work against and overcome the universal tendency towards decay, disorder, chaos, entropy—death, in a word.

Consider the analogy to human development, exhibited in the formation of the fetal brain, which can be seen as a sort of model for the process. When the fetus reaches the level of development at which it begins to produce brain cells, the cranium is little more than a thin shell surrounding an organic cellular fluid. The brain stem produces immature, undifferentiated cells, which take up their proper place in accord with the genetic pattern contained in the core of the human organism and its cellular components. These cells migrate into the cranium from the brain stem and then begin to divide. They don't, at this stage, have a specialized function. It is not until the cavity is full of cells, and they begin to extend their neuronal and glial connective tissue, that the process of specialization begins.

This process will result in the complex multitude of structures and functions that make the human brain such a marvelous creation. The child is born and the developmental process continues, with the brain becoming tuned to the environment, the mother, and the host of other stimuli that impinge upon it unceasingly. Gradually awareness dawns in the infant. It becomes ever more aware of its own needs and how to fulfill them.

The brain and body of the child interact with the world in a dynamic, ongoing way which will eventually lead to self-awareness, reflective thinking, and finally, a sense of separateness from the mother. Then comes a realization that it is possible to act independently to collect, store, and use energy in the form of food. Later, at maturity, the being can reproduce, and ultimately organize and regulate personal existence to create an individual life distinct from, yet fully interconnected with, the surroundings.

The planet, as a living system, is mirrored in miniature in the unending variety of every living system from the cell to the whole of the ecosystem, and is likewise gradually specializing, differentiating, and becoming ever more a distinct individual planet capable of running its own life in a way, and through processes, which supersede those of the various parts.

Teilhard de Chardin, the French archaeologist and mystic, suggested that the surface of the world will one day be completely covered by intelligence—what he termed the "noosphere." In order for this to happen all the basic parts must reach a dynamic steady state of development, and be fully interconnected at ever more complex, orderly, and efficient levels of organization. It then attains the ability to regulate the elements and resources of its own nature in an intelligent, conscious fashion. The structures and functions of the living planet are a marvelous creation like our own brains and bodies. Self-awareness and consciousness continue to grow as the earth develops its own distinct identity.

As we continue to install the fiber optic and satellite telecommunications system, we further bring about the "noosphere" Chardin spoke of. We all become ever more part of the global awareness and intelligence. The living system develops its overall individual nature based upon the subsystems of elemental compounds, organic chemicals, cells, organisms, species, cultures, etc. And we human beings are one of the more complex and highly developed mediums of self-awareness to come into being up to this time within the seething envelope of life on the skin of the world.

It is through living systems that the energy and elements of our living planet are organized and regulated. The planet becomes aware of itself through ever more orderly, complex and efficient forms of organization, and attempts to regulate its resources in such a way as to insure equitable distribution of essential nutriment to all forms which are part of its being. At the planetary level we humans are building the specialized elements of the brain of the planet, and we are the primary mediums of reflective self-awareness and global consciousness. The planet is alive, developing a mind of its own!

The brain and body of the world are growing ever more richly interconnected, especially through the medium of the fiber-optic tele-communications networks. The mind of the earth is manifest in us as the primary agents of its creation, and recreation. The planet aligns itself with the other bodies in the solar system and follows the path of balance and harmony therein, moving with minimal resistance through the heavens according to the needs of the greater whole. So we human beings must align ourselves with minimal resistance so as to equalize the flow of light through our interconnected circuitry, minimize impedance and resistance between our various parts, and learn to live and act in accord with the greater system we are part of: The Living Planet.

The Silicon Loop of Consciousness

It all started in the mud. Common clay may well be our most distant ancestor. After the body of the earth cooled and the oceans formed sediments which settled on the margins of the seas, and the atmosphere began to form, two of the most plentiful of the young planet's elements, aluminum and silicon were mixed together through the process called hydration. Over time, as the oceans rose and fell, vast deposits of aluminum silicate—clay—were left to dry and harden. This substrate became the medium for the gradual spread of life across the exposed surface of the world.

Research on the qualities and characteristics of clay indicate that it dries, and, at a certain specific point in the drying process it gives off bursts of gamma radiation. The energy of the sun is thus absorbed and its frequency transformed. In the process of absorbing and releasing radiation of various sorts, clay can form into the precursors of what biologists call lipids, which are the basic components of cell walls. The little spheres of silicon dioxide, with drops of ionized mineral water inside, organized themselves into microscopic energy transformers, and energy exchange in patterns began. Some scientists suggest this may have led to the eventual formation of organic life.

Energy in formation pulsed through the common clay, and, given the modern use of ceramics and computer chips, still does. It is obvious that minerals, which form the skin of the planet, have always played an important part in all of its functions. They are, by analogy, the primary medium of retaining information about what has happened over the lifetime of the earth. The geologic memory of the mineral strata is an important source of knowledge about the history of the world. The cellulose memory of trees tells us much about the processes of global growth and decay.

All inorganic and organic forms contain the salty mineral elements of the world in varying amounts. The interaction of minerals as they form into compounds is the result of the way the energies they contain relate to one another. This is called electromagnetic resonance in science, and without it compounds could not form, and molecular bonds could not be sustained. The energy that fills the universe and travels in waves, or stands still as particles, permeates and courses through the various matrices of what we perceive as inorganic and organic matter. This interactivity is the source of all creation.

As a living system the earth organizes itself into the multitude of materials and forms we experience as the natural world. It regulates itself by continually improving the way it collects, stores, transfers, and uses the energy of the sun. It grows ever more complex and differentiated in the process, giving rise to the delicate yet durable amino acid conversion units and communications systems known as living beings, among which we humans are the most complex. It has taken millions of years for our carbon-based brains to rise several feet above the mud, surround themselves with a mineral shell, support themselves on calcium "stilts," nourish themselves with oxygen through the iron-based medium of blood, and create the cultures and civilizations that are, by analogy, the thoughts of the planet itself. So it is that our crystalline minerals are essential components in life as we know it.

And now the consciousness that resides in our brains, the by-product of the millennia of development in the mud, is returning to the silicon matrix within which it was first contained. We are now storing what we know in systems composed of precious metals, various mineral and organic compounds, and silicon computer chips. And we are sending information around the world through silicon cables. Energy in formation is being transmitted via microwaves, radio waves, and other carriers across the personal, social, and political boundaries of the current geopolitical environment.

As we move through the next century, we shall see the earth surrounded in a net of glass fibers made of silicon, and of satellites made of precious metals. We have purified our clay, extracted the mineral substance that is as clear as pure water or gas, and that links every part of the globe together with every other. And through these fibers run the thoughts of a world in formation, growing, becoming more aware of its own identity and nature. Consciousness is expanding, intelligence is increasing, as ever richer interconnections are made and as the planet learns to talk to itself through the silicon-based telecommunications network.

There can be no overstatement of the importance of glass. It was essential in the development of the microscope and telescope, the manifest forms in the mineral elements of the lenses which allow us to send and receive signals far beyond the scope of our limited human sensory systems. The results of the spread of silicon-based technology will be a planet that is globally unified. Such a global entity has the capacity to become aware of itself, to communicate with itself digitally via cyberspace, unconcerned with space and time. There is an electronic continent, an energy frontier still to be fully explored and developed by the human organism.

We human beings are very specialized forms of cells, energy transformers of an amazing and marvelous sort. In our genetic codes are stored the plans for the most mysterious and powerful communications system that exists: the human organism itself. And it is through us that the earth is learning to talk to itself and become aware of itself as an individual, integrated, complete entity. We are of major importance in the growth process of a vast, intricate, living system. Our function in the evolution of our planet is to carry information that will allow the system to gain a more complex awareness, and a consequent ability to better organize and regulate its own nature and resources.

Layer upon layer the sediments are clarified and lain down on the earth. Now we are creating objects made of layers of rare minerals in space. These satellites, in orbiting the planet, improve both the clarity and scope of communications. Humanity has created a shell many miles thick in the upper atmosphere. Through probes beyond our world we have come to see what was once beyond knowing, and through the incredible invention of glass we have made telescopes to see to the further reaches of the universe, and into the depths of the molecule, the cell, the layers of our organism, and developed an awareness of the composition of stars like our sun, from which all the elements have come forth.

The six outer layers of the human brain grow ever more complex and orderly as they ascend towards the outer cortical surface. The more complex, orderly, and efficient the layer is, the more operations it can carry out at one time. The richer and more interconnected the structure of the tissue, the more channels along which information can be transmitted and received. Each layer is interconnected to those below and above, and the outer cortex is likewise interconnected to the limbic system and mid-brain. Thus are all the parts of the body joined together which make up the living system we each are.

This is much like the way the planet forms its global inter-connectivity. The difference is that in the planetary system the signals are of pure energy on a multitude of frequencies and bandwidths of the electromagnetic spectrum. The cognitive abilities of the planetary system are increasing proportionately as the layers ascend into the heavens.

The living earth reaches out in the process of seeking other living planets, of joining the interstellar and interplanetary elements of the universal mind into a coherent and self-aware whole. A shell of radiation one hundred light years across surrounds our world! We are a radiant little planet singing in the vastness of space.

We humans, due to our complexity, are aware that we are aware of ourselves being aware. Simple forms such as a leaf are aware of the sun in a rudimentary way. They have reactive awareness. More complex forms are aware of themselves, like lizards and insects, and act on their own volition. This is responsive awareness. Reactive awareness gives rise to self-activated responsive awareness. This second phase of awareness eventually gives rise, when sufficient complexity is achieved in a system, to the sort of reflective-awareness organisms such as we humans have, along with various other higher mammals. And when a system reaches a high enough level of order and complexity, when its feedback loops result in reflective capacity such as we have, then, according to Gregory Bateson, in his great work *Towards an Ecology of Mind*, we achieve the level defined as "mind." Mind can grow beyond this level, to planetary magnitude, and perhaps even further into the universal unified awareness of life and creation essential to a holistic view.

At this point consciousness becomes able to project itself around the world and across the heavens at the speed of light. It all began in the mud. It continues to grow through the medium of silicon, which is merely clarified mud, refined to purity. This was both the first container of energy in formation, and the final medium in the silicon loop of consciousness of which we are a part.

Scientific Shamanism

The man's face turns gradually bluer as the oxygen to his brain is cut off by the rope around his neck. The helpers who wait nearby watch, transfixed, as the Aleut shaman's body contorts and jerks in spasmodic undulation. Finally, at the last moment, after the shaman has lost consciousness, but just before he is dead, he is rapidly cut down, carried into a nearby hut, and laid out under ceremonial blankets. The chanting and singing begin, the gentle pulse of the drum, the rattle of the gourd, and songs of medicine. The helpers nod in mutual approval as they all know their leader is entering into the "world next to this one" to speak with spiritual beings and attempt, with all the strength and cleverness he has developed over a lifetime of fasting, deprivation, and prayers, to bring back from the nether worlds some sign, some piece of information, some oracular answer to the questions his people seek to answer.

They do this in order to better themselves, maintain their sense of individual and group identity, and live in harmony with the invisible forces that permeate their environment. They live in a universe described by the body of knowledge that comprises the world view of their culture and finds its deepest expression in the visions of the shaman.

A confused young man, an accomplished athlete, a one-time Christian, goes off alone into the woods and consumes a tiny piece of paper, or perhaps a handful of mushrooms, or a bag full of cacti. He is lonely, uncertain, afraid, and seeks some way out of his misery. He is a champion runner, but he has begun to lose competitions, for he is approaching his thirties, and has no idea what he will do with his life once the bottom falls out of his short-lived career as a professional athlete.

He has been depressed, unable to eat, communicate with others, or sleep well. After going back to church and finding the experience inadequate to his needs, he turned to his team advisers and found them sadly lacking in answers. He engaged in several months of sessions with a psychologist who helped quell the tortuous turnings of his mind temporarily. But all of these attempts to find balance have failed to show him alternatives or to keep the mind from reasserting its confusion when he does not go to the sessions. So he turns to mind alteration using psychotropic plants as a possible alternative.

What he does is dangerous. It could cost him his sanity or his life. But he feels anything would be better than what he has been experiencing. He feels like he is at war with himself. He walks through the woods waiting for the effects of the mind alterant to overcome him and throw him suddenly into another world where all things are transformed and the answers he is seeking just might be found. He lies down on a patch of moss in the dappled shade and feels himself enter into a journey which will carry him into the depths of the labyrinth of his own mind, then kick him out the other side with a different view of things.

When he comes down from the experience, he is shaken, but satisfied. He has seen that there are alternatives, and that he does have a world of choices available to him that were not visible before. He knows, after he talks with those experienced in such activities, that what has been revealed will in itself not change his life. He knows that now he must attempt to realize his vision and act on the alternatives he has seen.

It is midnight in the laboratory. The middle-aged scientist sits before his computer terminal staring transfixed into the amber glow of the video screen. He takes another drink from his coffee cup to stimulate his nerves, another puff of his cigarette to steady his hands after being up for twenty-two hours in search of an answer to the problem he is attempting to tackle. His career depends upon his finding the answer to the complex set of equations in front of him before anyone else. The exhausted team of assistants and lab workers with whom he has been working dream fitfully in their beds knowing they are on the verge of a great discovery.

Our problem solver has not eaten for two days. As he stares into the screen, he begins to doze off and at last, bodily reserves consumed by fatigue, he falls into a semi-conscious state where his mind continues to wrestle with the problem. Out of the dim welter of confusion emerges a startling symbol which, if added into the equations on his screen, will solve the problem. He is shocked back into conscious awareness, uses the new variable, draws on some hidden reserve of energy and completes his work. His co-workers find him there in the morning where he has collapsed and entered into a deep, dreamless sleep from which he emerges refreshed, when the cheers of the lab workers fill the air proclaiming he has found the answer to the riddle which they have labored to solve.

Shamanism is not dead. It has been with us at least fifty thousand years. The ones selected by, or forced by, culture to enter into an altered state to seek answers to pressing questions must still undergo training, initiation, and learn to interpret the results of their vision seeking. The means of entering into altered states are various, ranging from near-death asphyxiation, to mind-altering chemicals, to computer reverie. There are as many means as there are people, but all exist for a single purpose. They help us find answers and deepen our understanding of ourselves, and the world we live in.

The shaman must be educated, trained, and tempered. Then he, or she, must undergo progressively more difficult initiations into the nature of the problems to be answered, and of the puzzles to be solved in order to more adequately define the elements of individual and group experience and identity in need of clarification. The shaman enters into the "other world" that is beyond the visible one most share, in order to reconstruct perception and cognition. In the spirit world, he can regenerate the agreed upon mass hallucination termed "culture" by those who need terms. He can reunify and integrate the individual and group identity in a new order. The shaman then undergoes testing by the inhabitants and forces of that nether realm and, if found worthy, is allowed to return to the people with an answer that will benefit the group and enhance his, or her, personal status in the community.

Whether we consider the shaman of the hunter-gatherers, the priest of the agricultural communities, or the scientist of the computer and information age, we are dealing with an analogous role, a common social function, a necessary job. All cultures need the general synthesizer, the creative mythologist spoken of by Joseph Campbell, who can discover within the "unexpected universe" beneficial answers to crucial questions. The fusion process they use to create generates new information. This information will help overcome that fission of the critical masses of human potentials which can cause disintegration of identity, culture, and, ultimately, civilization.

The shaman is not dead. The shaman is needed now more than ever. Those who perform this function in modern society have simply adopted a new set of formulations and practices whereby to deal with a reality no one really ever expected or knew about. These new ideas can be collectively defined as the basis for what is called herein "Hologenics"—a set of conceptions that generates a sense of wholeness within the individual, the community, the nation, and the world.

The shaman now seeks to discern the thoughts of a universal mind in formation among us, and within us. He receives the collective dreams of his people. By extension he entertains those of the species as a whole as we seek to live together in a world fast approaching the limits of growth, and the threshold of a new state of being, identity, and existence on a global scale. It is crucial that this be done. Otherwise chaos will be our inheritance, and disintegration our fate.

Towards a Planetary Mind

By now it should be clear. The world is developing a mind of its own, and we are but a part, albeit a very important part, of it. The ramifications of this analogy are stunning. It can aid us in understanding what we are, what our purpose is, the meaning inherent in our lives, and numerous others aspects of our existence in this world. And the idea is not without practical application.

Take, for instance, a joint project of the Chinese government and the East-West Center in Hawai'i. Together they are attempting to map the complete water table of the Chinese mainland. The purpose of this project is to equalize the distribution of water throughout the lands in order that everyone from farmer to urban government official shall have enough, and at the right times. The arid western regions of the United States have been so mapped over this century, dams built, canals constructed, regulatory policies put in force, creating one of our major growth regions. Ecological awareness is one way the human mind assists the planet in its growing self-consciousness, by helping it regulate and organize its resources and distribution systems. By equalizing these systems natural disasters such as flood and drought can be averted, or at least minimized. Conflicts resulting from inequitable distribution of resources and services can be calmed. The ravages of famine, disease, and poverty can be mitigated.

We human beings are being forced to adapt to an ever more complex world, becoming continually more richly connected with each other as peoples, cultures, and nations. If we are to survive and have reason to hope we can salvage the future, we must join in the process of emerging planetary consciousness.

Biologist Gregory Bateson noted the beginnings of what he called "an ecology of mind." The great philosopher Dane Rudhyar speaks, as do many, of the "global man," the "man of plenitude," the "globalization of consciousness," and Paul Tillich describes the "new being" who is gradually emerging from the plethora of localized, conflicting interests which have marked human history throughout the modern ages. The cyclic patterns of growth are approaching the next synthesis, and as the consciousness of man and planet become one, the old fixed boundaries upon which we now build and order our lives are falling away. This great shift is at the root of our global identity crisis, and we can either embrace it or prepare to go the way of the dinosaurs.

The processes Bateson describes as "mind" are universal. Julian Jaynes noted that the universe seems less like a great machine, and more like a great idea. Mind develops as the elements unite and form the universe, galaxies, solar systems, planets, life forms, and awareness as it extends from the micro to the macro cosmic.

It is thus imperative that we each develop a planetary mind on our way to becoming aware of the universal mind. We must "think globally, and act locally." We must see ourselves as a part of the living planet, or we will face our end apart from it, alone, alienated, isolated, and cut off from the vital forces at the very core of life.

These essays are a lyrical exploration of the murky depths and brilliant heights of the world identity during this time of transition. We are moving from the part to the whole, from the individual self to the global self, from mechanism to holism, from machine to information system, from atoms to photons. They present a variety of analogies, metaphors, alternative views, and studied opinions regarding the experience of human life within the new context of the living systems of our increasingly conscious planet.

We must see the patterns of life in this world with new eyes, learn to hear the vast concert that is the symphony of life itself, which often seems beyond our ability to understand, with new ears. As our consciousness develops more coherency, as our lives become enriched with the complexity of modern experience, our identity crisis might be brought to an end.

This book, a few scribblings on cellulose, a complex of signals within computer circuits, is but a few more pages added to the longer book of our perpetual beginnings. It is an inquiry into the nooks and crannies of our earthly lives and our evolving awareness within the universal mind.

Planetary Thoughts

"These are the words of the planet, these eyes are the eyes of the planet, and these ears are the ears of the planet." So said Dr. Joseph Campbell as he looked intently into the camera during an interview with Bill Moyers in 1987. He went on to say that we must recognize that our bodies, and hence ourselves, are made of this planet, and it is through us that it lives a part of its life. Also, America in particular is suffering in terms of not having a myth that is shared by all, and which gives the nation, as a whole, its meaning in life. Campbell said that the next myth must be planetary in nature, and that it must transcend nation, religion, race, and the many other characteristics that are, when considered alone, divisive and fragmentary.

Earlier I pointed out that a mind must organize random inputs on a variety of wavelengths into meaningful formations. The mind perceives patterns and makes representations of them internally which, when spoken or written, become language, and the means by which we can shape the material tools we use to "make" the world we experience. It is these patterns of activity based upon our sensations, perceptions, and inner responses that are transformed into language and the systems of communication upon which our communities are based. And it is no less true on the global level.

All that we experience, the trees, the land forms, the objects, creatures, people, and so on, are, by analogy, the thoughts of our living planet. We are, as Fritjof Capra in *The Turning Point* says, "embedded" in this world, and are the repository of the thoughts, dreams, imagination, memory, and creativity for the planet in many ways. We don't live on the earth—we are involved in the process of its creation and live in it. We are part of the process of creation within its mind. It is through us that the world works towards the goal of finding ever more orderly and complex ways and means of organizing its energies and regulating its resources.

The earth, in turn, is but a minuscule thought-form in the solar, galactic, and intergalactic mentality or creative process that makes up the universal mind, and which resembles a great thought more than a great machine. We humans are far less important than we think, but far more important than we imagine. We are, by analogy, the "cells" which combine to make up the mind of the planet. We are major functionaries in a cognitive planet, engaged in the process of creating planetary thoughts.

We exist as the most complex, differentiated form of being. We are the only organism that has gotten beyond the receptive, reactive and merely reflective levels of being. On the receptive level we have rocks, water, air, and other substances that are receptive in nature. They absorb the diffuse radiation and random energies of the sun and change them, re-radiating them as heat.

On the reactive level are the simplest organisms from the single cell forms to life in the vegetable kingdoms. In the animal kingdom reactivity is expressed in such simple creatures as snails, lizards, and various insects. The next level of being is clearer, rarer and, more reflective. Just a few human organisms are endowed with the capacity to think and make choices as to how they live, where they go, and how they fulfill their purpose in a world beyond instinct, and without borders or boundaries.

But at this level of complexity we humans are the only organism with projective consciousness. We alone can create patterns of activity in our minds and project them onto the lower levels of materials and organisms in such a way as to recreate our thoughts as objects, information and societies.

The "objective" reality we see around us is nothing more or less than a projection of what we ourselves contain. We are microcosms of the universe, and have the capacity which Bateson described as "mind"— which is here defined as multi-level awareness that is aware of itself being aware that it is aware of itself being aware. This multi-layered reflectivity is the basis of our unique consciousness. And we have the further capacity to extend our consciousness beyond ourselves, into the planetary level of awareness wherein the interconnectivity and unity between all things becomes more than obvious—it becomes apparent, expansive, and reaches out to the very stars to find and prove itself.

It's as if the planet were reaching out, through our space probes, our wave communications systems, and our projections of ourselves onto the Moon, Mars, and beyond—as if the very consciousness of the planet were expanding into the cosmos seeking more of itself wherever it might be found. A sphere of electromagnetic radiation surrounds us, almost a hundred light years across!

And it reaches inward as well, seeking to extend itself into the most microcosmic aspects and parts of itself, the organisms, cells, molecules, atoms, nuclei, and immaterial forms of radiation at the very heart of life. Life begins and ends in light, from the photon to the quasar and back. We are becoming a "cognitive" planet, one that is fully aware of itself because all of its parts are joined in unitary awareness of their interconnectivity, which is eternal, and infinitely diverse. Such phenomena as UFOs, ghosts, and a host of other things mysterious and odd can be seen in a different light when looked at from this perspective. They are all planetary thoughts, aspects of a global sensibility that is our destiny and future to recognize and understand, if we are to have any future at all.

Thoughts Like Flocks of Birds

The thoughts that form in our minds, like those of the planet such as cities, forests, and the atmosphere, or those of the heavens like solar systems, galaxies, and super-clusters, remind me of flocks of birds. One evening I was sitting next to the river watching the water flow and suddenly saw what looked liked a sheet of silver foil appear and disappear in the air! At first I couldn't tell what it was, but when I saw the phenomena again, I determined it was a flock of starlings flitting through the rich golden twilight. When they all changed direction as one, the evening glow reflecting from their backs looked like a sheet of silver for a moment. Each small bird alone was little more than speck in the vision, but when the whole bunch of them twisted and turned their collective shine made a startling impression on my eye because of their overall pattern of unified action.

Similar environments and experiences give rise to similar patterns of activity, whether it be for cells, birds, people, or thoughts. Individual beings, and the groups they form are, of course, quite different from one another, but when they work together to form a whole that is greater than the sum of their parts, they truly shine. The patterns of their combined activities are expressions of their inherent meanings in the environment as an integrated, whole, living system.

The gradual homogenization of culture on a planetary scale, brought about by the increasingly rich interconnections between the people and the communications technologies which they use, has led to a consistency of conditions and experiences from which we can see emerging similar patterns of thoughts. These are reflections of the possibilities inherent in the global system as it becomes ever more integrated, orderly, complex, and efficient.

What is interesting about how similar thoughts arise from similar environments and experiences is that thinkers all across the world tend to often arrive at the same conclusions almost simultaneously. Take the case of Darwin and Wallace and the theory of natural selection. Both men arrived at the same conclusions without having met one another— but they had encountered similar conditions in their research and travels, which led them to coincidentally act as hosts for this seminal theory.

Simultaneity of thought is especially evident in the realm of scientific research. More and more we are seeing the Nobel Prize shared by several scientists who have been working on the same ideas in isolation, but who have come to the same results in unison. This has been going on for a long time, but is becoming more commonplace as science and technology spread. In order to use a technology one must adapt a specialized language, which in turn alters perceptions, and brings those who use that language into a commonly held view of the problems and solutions to be dealt with and discoveries to be made.

After Darwin composed his theory of evolution by natural selection, he put it in a drawer for many years afraid that he would be heavily criticized for the views he put forth. It was not until Wallace came to the same conclusions and was about to publish them that Darwin felt compelled to publish his findings in order to retain primacy for his discovery—he shared the credit as a true scientist and gentleman is disposed to do. Simultaneous occurrence of ideas is a natural outcome of activities within the mind of an integrated living system.

The tree of life that is the living tissue of our brain, when developed to a certain point, and in specific ways, becomes host for complex systems of information that can lead to the discovery of innovations and inventions that affect us all. Individual thoughts, like small birds, flock together, move in a unified way, shine together like a silver sheet of shimmering unity, and come to roost in the environment of a prepared and receptive mind.

Probable thoughts exist as potentialities within the mind-culture-environment matrix. When they take on particular form and join together, they are, by analogy, like the specific flocks of birds that inhabit selected ecosystems. When the birds find conditions such as weather, food sources, and nesting sites that are suitable and which satisfy their instinctual needs, they go about the process of nesting, mating, reproducing, and rearing offspring therein.

Thoughts are like this also. When they find appropriate minds, the trees of life, to alight in, they do so, and therein they begin to join together in song, life, and growth. A particular thought might land in any number of similarly developed brains around the world, find expression in a wide variety of symbol systems, and ultimately find a form of expression, an offspring if you will, which can spread, enter into the collective mind through symbol, technic, or behavior. The flock spreads, extends it range, grows more common, adapts to variations in the environments encountered, and finally becomes an integral part of the ecosystem which it then fills to the limits.

Sparrows are one such bird. Machines are another. But I prefer the starlings, whose backs shine in the setting sun, that silver flock which, in moving together, becomes something more than the parts, which shines and sends a bright, surprising message to the startled onlooker and, on recognition, leads to a fullness of understanding and appreciation of nature that is evidence of that deeper unity which is in turn so hard to see. Yet it is so evident within us, about us, and beyond us into the far reaches of the heavens.

Superstructures of the Imagination

"Ordering potentials" shape every message, or process, in the mind. They signify associations and the multi-level meanings of the combined effect of any given signal on overall mental activity. As the mind becomes clear, it is easy to see the ways things are interconnected. There is no doubt that the combined effects of our minds are realized in the form of thoughts which motivate action, shape the world and order its potentials into chosen forms.

The emotive tonalities, or musical aspect of spoken language, which shape the final meaning of the message being considered, are the ordering potentials in our case. Ordering potentials determine what comes forth and what remains unmanifest, and they shape the ultimate form of any given set of systemic structures and processes. An example of a deeply ingrained ordering potential is that of the rules of grammar and syntax. These influence the degree of redundancy and meaning in the messages riding a carrier wave. Triggers and gates in the mind respond to familiar signals and cause firing patterns to occur in the neuronal tissue. These patterns are compared to stored patterns conditioned into easy recognition through constant repetition in the form of memory.

To be aware of such potentials, and to control them, and to thus affect perceptions in others by modulating the signal in such a way as to lower resistance, is to discover a fantastic tool for moving in this world of ionized polarities. The sum of the vectors formed by internal neuron firing patterns is thus defined by the limits to which each signal goes before it reaches its point of extinction. This is the basic form of any given thought. Such neurological patterns are given cognitive, linguistic tags, called words, which form the boundaries of each being's experience. Language is a sort of positive filtering system, only allowing in that which conforms to the cultural memory. Ordering potentials are thus the superstructures of the imagination.

These overriding patterns of activity are most often subliminal and felt more than known. The degree to which one is exceptional is directly proportionate to the degree to which one can access the superstructures via the limbic system. The higher cortical areas then read the combined emotional tone and language of speech, and connect these to higher areas and forms of activity that supersede the individual and are global in scope, and universal in formation. This more expansive understanding of the combined inputs is often tagged as intuitive sensitivity, or even mislabeled "psychic."

Those who bear the genetic message (which is an ordering potential in the biological realm) for high degrees of intuitive sensitivity have great potential value to self and others and world. They are usually chosen through cultural selection for special positions and functions within the collective mind of society. They order the mind of the young, or master the arts of projecting illusions, reordering materials, controlling economic systems, etc.

In a very real sense we access the superstructures used in thought through the use of the "technology" of language. Image, sound, sensations of various sorts relate in a super-conscious form of activity that allows the system to communicate with itself and monitor all of its functions. Reverie, dreams, and imagination are the traditional means used to express new patterns of thought as we develop a planetary mind.

Creative activity of any sort reduplicates super-structural activity on the conscious level of awareness. Only a certain small percentage of the population will have the genetic markers and subsequent training which allows access to the superstructures and thus facilitates the highest orders of expression and accomplishment for, and throughout, the greater whole. Those who have such markers are but a chosen few, and their genetic patterns are maximally adaptive, made to become active when time and tide demand.

Those who are so gifted, able to utilize the superstructures of the imagination, are those capable of creating new paradigms or products that can change the face of civilization. Their minds are depolarized in certain areas and the flow of current across the neurons is equalized and rectified, with high amplitude and low impedance, allowing new thought forms to come into clearer focus. They can see answers where others see only a void. They make bright the way leading to a change of state. They alter the collective ordering potentials and express a redefined, regenerated human nature.

Such people can lead us into new worlds. Artists, scientists, theologians, philosophers, and others of the creative sort can see the world, as it will be, rather than only as it is. The new world order some speak of already exists for these people. They can extrapolate into the future, with unreal accuracy in their seemingly prophetic utterances.

What do they see between now and then? Crisis will occur before reformation of the planetary system. The population will peak and force humanity to slough off many unsuitable peoples, primarily those who cannot adapt to the chaos inherent in change. Then in time the systemic whole shall be regenerated into a coherent, integrated form with a more unified consciousness, and a lasting, enduring identity. This is our future. We shall know who we are as individuals, as a people, and as a world unified within the universal mind.

One means of bringing this future into the present is through creating a new way of looking at ourselves, at living and dying in the 21st century, and at the universe around us. It is in formation now, even as you read this. It has been emerging for decades as the environmental and social elements have become more interconnected. As transportation, telecommunications, and other advanced technologies have spread, many people have opened their minds to new possibilities.

Through the use of planetary-mindedness and hologenic language, we can reorganize and regenerate our worldview so as to bring our thoughts and actions into coherent unity. We are becoming able to reform our world view in accordance with ordering potentials evident in emerging superstructures that more adequately reflect what we are actually seeing and doing. We must get to the bottom of our dilemma and reconstruct ourselves. This requires that we consider ourselves anew— our communities, our world, and the universe in which we are embedded.

It is time to understand the meaning of immortality, magic, mind, and nature, free of the limiting views of the past. We cannot, nor do we even need to, give up our traditions and that within us that is of value. However, we need to recreate our perceptions, refine our language, and regenerate our identity so as to be integrated within the greater whole. Let us thus proceed to further develop our global awareness and connect ourselves to the universal mind.

II

The World Body

THERE ARE SOME WHO ARGUE that our planet is not "alive" at all, for it cannot reproduce. But who is able to define just what life is? Is a virus alive? This is a matter still being debated. Whether or not it is alive, it certainly plays a part in the lives of human beings. So, whether or not the planet is actually alive in accord with our limited ability to make such a determination is not so important as the fact that it contains us. We are most certainly what we think of as alive, and our civilization as a body is alive.

In political terms we are seeing continuing references to the "world body" in reference to the local, national, and international entities that compose our civilization. These various cells of organized activity interrelate through the telecommunications network and have begun to act in concert when there is a threat to the well-being of the parts, such as in Somalia, Iraq, Bosnia, etc. And how can we have a body without mind? This is not possible. There must be the equivalent of a mind. The mind organizes the cells of the body and governs their relationships and communications processes. But this mind is not of the same sort, or of the same order, as that of individuals or cultures.

Like the mind of the infant, the planetary mind has an innate character apart from the conditioning it receives from the local, immediate surroundings. Our civilization is alive, and it is intelligent, seeking a way to look at the world that we can share, that can be agreed upon in its general outlines. Then the mind can develop awareness of its own existence apart from its source, and create an identity of its own.

31

We are dependent upon and attached to our earth. We live within it, and in order to survive we must, as an infant must, develop a healthy relationship with our own being, others, and the world around us. We must see the world body as our own. We require bonds of affection to live, reproduce, and to appreciate our experience. Relationships and feelings are the essence of, and the foundation for, the knowledge we absorb. Through our interactive participation in the life of the mind, we are enriched and able to give our attention to the needs of others.

Equitable, rectified distribution of goods, services, and energy must be the basis for our laws, institutions, and interactions. The rules by which the body is governed must be agreeable in order for us to develop our organizational potentials and performance efficiency. In the process we must stabilize our populations at a sustainable level in accord with the basic laws that govern our ability to produce and share resources.

When we ignore the laws of our world body, the results are expressed in the forms of overpopulation, pollution, disease, death-dealing conflicts, and changes in the elemental balance of nature. Overpopulation exposes us to those sickening elements in nature we create to power our fission-driven civilizations, which alter the environment we are exposed to. The mutagens and pathogens we create in our nuclear reactors lead to mutations and aberrations on every level of life. They detract from the health of the body and lead to biological pathogens like cancer and AIDS, or to neuro-linguistic, or information, "viruses." All are at worst deadly to the body, unbalancing to the mind, distressing to the emotions, and damaging to our health.

The world body and mind are our own. We must care for them, ourselves and our life—the precious life that we will lose if we do not take care to sustain it. The more this recognition spreads and leads to political and social action, the better our chances of survival and the more fulfilling our quality of life. With our needs taken care of, we are then free to explore our choices and take those paths we choose to facilitate our development and maintain our lives.

Though it may be true that all is light, all is connected, and that our individual lives are but passing figments of the imagination of the universal and planetary minds, it is nevertheless important to come to understand our place in the world, as individuals and cultures, and to live in harmony with it. This is the means to a renewed sense of wholeness; a stretching of self beyond individualism, into the "we" that is in formation globally. The real question is not merely, who am I? This question cannot actually be answered, as the truth of our source is silent and ineffable. The question is, who are we? We are all one. We are the human beings. We are part of the greater whole. We are not separated or divided. We are joined in the great circle of life and any feeling of being apart from the whole is an emanation of the divisions inherent in ego, of the illusory self that is but a convenience.

We are living beings, part of a living world, of a living cosmos, and as such there is only life and one soul. Death is a denial of the facts inherent in the physical laws governing the conservation of mass and energy. Nothing can be destroyed. Only our limited sense of self can expire, and the self is but a veil to protect us from our true Self, which is immortal and infinite, which is who we truly are.

The Regenerative Planet

Many journal articles critical of the Gaia Hypothesis suggest the planet cannot be considered alive even though it meets three of the four criteria required of living beings. But perhaps this isn't so. It has been further theorized by some astrophysicists and astronomers that, on occasion the Earth, as with every sphere, collides with an object that breaks it up. This can be occasioned by a piece of the moon falling into our oceans in the literal sense, or if an unpredicted wandering planetoid, asteroid or meteor strikes up a relationship of the most intimate sort with our lovely mother earth.

A large hunk of ice or rock from outer space comes along and it just breaks the planet's resistance down. It enters into the atmosphere like a sperm entering an egg. The inner body of the planet is seeded thereby with interstellar dust, organic materials and stimulating substances. The earth is broken apart for a time then reassembles itself into a renewed world to begin its life again. Is it just gravity? Or is it love? The mother regenerates a new body, new possibilities, while carrying remnants of the mate within as the suitor's stray dust vaporously makes its way back into the skies. This interstellar "sperm" truly makes a lasting impression on the world we live within.

But the odds of this happening make it a long time between celestial dates, and an even longer time between a merger of sky mates. The time scale is beyond us, as we have only just been in the world long enough to start to wake up and remember where we are from, and discover where it is likely we are bound. So perhaps the world reproduces, and is alive in ways, and on a scale beyond our frail imaginations—and perhaps we are the earth's own dream of itself waking up to a new love's face in the morning skies.

Energy and Disease

There have admittedly been enormous advances in medicine over the last few hundred years. The development of the germ theory led to a profound shift in our perception of disease mechanisms that resulted in the near extinction of some of mankind's most virulent illnesses. Inoculation and immunology have brought about, in part, both preventative measures that remain in force for a lifetime in the former case, and awareness of the effects of all manner of external factors on human resistance to disease in the latter.

Stress, pollutants, radiation of various sorts—all can play a part in weakening the resistance of the body leading to a failure of the immune system. When this system fails, the body becomes confused, unable to sharply define the boundary between what is safe relating to the self and what is dangerous in relating to other than self. Usually the body is flexible and tolerant of the myriad host of wandering bacteria and viruses it encounters. But when the system is out of balance, "dis-ease" results.

Ayurvedic medicine in India maintains that, in fact, identity and immunity are one and the same thing. Knowing what one is not is the basis of identity. What remains is what, or who, one is. A branch of medicine has emerged in the U.S. called "holistic medicine" which takes much the same stance, taking the position that, if the underlying conditions of a person's life that contribute to imbalance are not dealt with, then the use of techniques aimed at ridding the body of foreign entities will ultimately prove futile. Organisms which reproduce and proliferate due to a weakened immune system cause disease and surround us all the time. In fact, they inhabit us.

Our bodies carry a full complement of viruses, bacteria, and other microorganisms that are benign in the healthy body, but deadly to one who is weakened. The Navajo people believe that disharmony within the person precedes sickness, and that this must be dealt with, to prevent spread of the illness, through ceremonial healing chants, drumming, sand paintings, and the use of medicinal plants. The spread of illness leads, if unchecked, to ever worsening conditions that can extend themselves beyond the individual into society. Others become sick as well, threatening the community as a whole.

The AIDS virus is one such culprit—a social virus that just loves people to death. It is, in and of itself, harmless. But when it is able to weaken the immune system by tricking it into attacking its host body, simple colds, flu-like symptoms, coughs, and other apparently innocuous conditions multiply and spread. These are warning signs that the body is becoming weak in response to the variety of stressful agents mentioned above. It is when these lesser conditions continue and worsen that the real trouble begins. Then a major disease can take root, such as pneumonia, which can kill. Ironically, those few who are exposed to the HIV virus without contracting the illness are those who simply don't respond to it with an outpouring of immune systems forces. Without the proliferation of immune factors the virus cannot reproduce, remains inert, cannot kill.

The hanta virus is another example. Its deadly spread had to do with environmental conditions that facilitated the increased spread of rodents and their excrement among some human populations. The symptoms appeared suddenly, killed rapidly, and were difficult to understand at first. The Navajo would probably suggest the lack of balance brought this about, while the allopathic physician would lay the blame squarely on the virus itself. They are both probably right.

The vast concert of our bodily systems is some of the most complex and delicate music in the world. These systems are, in their way, incredibly strong and flexible. The body, in spite of all that humans do to foul it and destroy it, remains aloof, almost seeming to laugh at how we try to actually destroy ourselves. However, when our finely tuned organisms are thrown out of synchrony, when one part is out of key or tune, so to speak, the whole concert degrades into chaos, eventually leading, in accord with the laws of entropy, to death if not corrected. We are thermodynamic entities, no less than any other part of the solar system, planetary biosphere, local ecosystems, communities, and organisms. We are living, embodied energy—electromagnetism on foot. We are electrified mud puddles spreading over the whole surface of the planet, carrying our microscopic accompanists, in all their singing grace, into every niche in nature.

From the moment of conception the unique energy that is the individual interacts in a complex resonant harmony with all of nature. These universal processes of creation are so vast, so intricate as to be comprehensible in only the most general terms. There is an intelligent vitality that causes the organism to grow, differentiate, and become ever more complex, orderly, and efficient in direct opposition to all probability. The symmetrical development of living forms depends first upon the sun, then upon the earth, then upon air, water, and food taken in during the pursuit of staying alive. This energy is broad spectrum electromagnetism. The multitudes of orderly material forms live in the most blatant interdependence, in a subtle network that is planetary in scope. Whole galaxies shiver in beautiful spirals, spheres and other forms expressive of the intergalactic unity of our "local" neighborhood.

Albert Einstein said that, "We often suffer from a sort of optical delusion. We act as if we are not connected to everything and everybody. We think we can separate ourselves from people who are different. We think that we are not connected to life in all its forms. It is the most painful delusion in the world today." The pain of this delusion can distort the human system so as to bring about a host of debilitating conditions. We sometimes live in such a pathological relationship to ourselves, others, and nature, in such disease-friendly environments—swollen, polluted urban areas especially—that our sense of harmony and connectivity cannot help but be diminished and provide favorable conditions for the spread of disease.

The ovum and sperm that join in creation are the conveyors of enough energy in meaningful formations to bring about the explosion of life and reproduce human intelligence under all manner of varied conditions. It is said that, if the energy of a single human body were to be released all at once, it could level a whole city! All things seek to recreate, to survive and to maintain the environment within which they live and grow.

This has been going on for many billions of orbits around the sun. The fertile egg and the eager sperm do a fantastic microscopic dance that is still a mystery to the most brilliant of investigators. Literally millions of sperm will gather around the ovum, but it only lets one inside to spark the reproductive sphere, the locked cell of life, to multiply and divide and grow. No one yet knows what criteria the ovum uses as a basis for this choice. But it is not inconceivable to imagine that she surveys the minute courtship motions and chooses in most cases the chemically sweetest, physically strongest candidate from among the dancing multitudes knocking at her atmosphere.

On the sub-molecular level the ovum and the sperm are generators of complex electromagnetic fields which must fuse, mesh, and interact in order for the information they contain to create the vast orchestra of the living, healthy, human being. The DNA and RNA they contain probably carry more information than the entire telecommunications network of the human race. Even when the human information-processing network includes all the libraries, books, and memories stored on the surface of our world, and all the electromagnetic bandwidths used for microwave, radio, short wave and long wave frequencies, it still adds up to only a part of the whole complex of information. Our organism continues to develop in a slightly less than random fashion. This defeats entropy through a dynamic process of non-equilibrium steady state. All of our history and future are contained in the genes of the sperm and the ovum, which are eternal. All that we have been and ever will become are enfolded into the micro-universes within them.

Our own brains are minute models of the external universe in which they are embedded. The universal mind and intelligence extends itself through the brain and into the world through materials and technologies to become a stable, manifest entity. It contains, in potential, enough connections to create in the material realms adaptations of and to the environment which have allowed us to survive millions of years under a wide variety of conditions. The brain will allow us, if we use our intelligence, our mind properly, to continue on for millions more. As long as the sun shines, the energy, flexibility, and information we contain is available for our survival.

We are, in fact, the primary medium for the most complex patterns of mind in operation in our living planet. All that we become through the marvelous processes and patterns of activity generated by the orchestras of our cells creates in the mineral, plant, and animal realms a solid basis for the development of self-aware human and global intelligence. We are the mind of the planet. It is through us the world sees itself. And it is our function to act in such a way as to create self-awareness on a planetary scale in order that the mind of the living earth can continue to develop the ability to organize and regulate itself as any animate entity must do to remain healthy.

What we need is to operate in harmonious ways, discerned through our intelligent self-awareness, with the energy that permeates and vitalizes the biosphere, the solar system, and the cosmos. This vital force is what holds things together—whether we call it life, gravity, or love—and keeps them healthy. It is what allows us to become ever more efficient, to continue to reproduce, to play our small parts in the harmonic composition of life. The energy that is in formation in the core of our cells must have a finely tuned instrument of expression in the material, manifest form of the organism, just as the music on the conductor's page must have a finely tuned orchestra of instruments to play the composer's creation.

The conductor is the vital force. The music is written in the DNA and RNA of the ovum and sperm. The orchestra is made up, by analogy, of the many instruments of the human body. Many organs and multitudes of microorganisms in dynamic interaction create the vast and delicate music that is life. Our bodies are the material expression of the electromagnetic network we are embedded within like so many notes on a cosmic page.

When we are out of tune in our lifestyles, foods, industry, and energy generation, there will be disharmony—which we experience as disease. In this state the communications channels will carry distorted information that can lead to a weakening of our identity, our sense of what is and is not who we are. Then come either mutations that cause us to crumble, or the failure of our immune systems, proliferation of disease, and, ultimately, death—cellular, personal, cultural, perhaps even planetary. Then comes the inevitable and complete breakdown into chaos of our energy fields and bodies, the final rush towards entropy and ultimate rest—"heat death" as the physicists call the state.

But I prefer to maintain confidence in the intelligence of the cell, the individual, the culture, the planet and the universe. I hold to the position that the innate intelligence of our vital forces will throw out what is not in harmony with a balanced sense of identity. The immune system cells surround and consume those factors within our bodies that are disruptive or lethal.

I believe the peoples, cultures, and nations of our planet will likewise use the information, intelligence, and communications systems we have created to join together in an effort to dispose of all those who are not a part of us, who will not enter into a shared understanding and live in harmony with the rest. Those who fail to be a part of the whole being cannot be allowed to proliferate.

We need to reach the highest possible level of performance and efficiency if we wish to continue on in this world. An intelligent planet will not allow anything less. We do not have to know how to play all the instruments, nor even how to read the music. We must simply know how to improvise our part of the jazz in such a way as to play our part in the global orchestra in a healthy way. The harmonized energy will spread as we eat, live, and behave in the ways that are best for all and will lead to a good result. Disease can be minimized and health insured, and our world can continue to grow in such a way that the basic needs of all are met.

Disease and the Planetary Mind

We change the world. The world changes us. Natural disaster, disease, and war are three of the earth's most effective population levelers. These factors affect our ability to communicate with ourselves, with others, and with the environment. Our identities weaken and our personal, cultural, or natural systems enter into the turbulent stages of transformation that inevitably precede a change of state. Systems undergoing a change of state always give off noise, or energy that is not information, which is incoherent. That noise is often perceived as excessive heat or pressure or static, such as that given off by volcanoes, infections, and countries preparing for war.

In order for the planet to create a coherent identity, with a stability and structural integrity that is both strong and flexible, all systems must be operating in such a way as to be at tension without being destructive. We must have tension in order to grow, to maintain movement, to insure optimum differentiation and diversity. In this way the various parts of the planetary system each retain special adaptive resistances that protect them, so that in the event one part of the population is destroyed, others will remain. But in order to prevent insanity in the planetary mind, global mental illness, and a subsequent universal collapse of human cultures and civilization into chaos and disorder—which could well result in extinction—all parts must work together for the benefit of the greater whole. The sense of coherent identity must permeate the whole living system in such a way as to insure our good health.

We can continue our existence only if we adapt to changes within and without ourselves, our cultures, and our environment. Often the way we live results in devastating effects we are not able to foresee or predict. City life provides conditions that foster the spread of AIDS (and before that bubonic plague, malaria, flu, and other diseases). Increasing complexity without increasing consciousness or efficiency results in distortions and delusions entering into our planetary mind, our living systems of communication and interaction, which can be deadly.

But we must always remember that disease is a result of imbalance in the system. It is a weakening of the greater whole, a loss of integrity, a lessening of the ability to organize and regulate the systems. The resulting inability to adapt leads to sickness, the eventual loss of consciousness. We cannot all be alike, cannot see things completely the same. We don't really want that, for it would limit our adaptive capacity—but we can see that dividing our self in ways that prevent the free flow of information, goods and services is a form of global insanity.

Disease is an adaptive response to the pressure and heat, the incoherence of a disorderly, static-filled environment at some level or other. At times, disease must enter into the system in order to force the flushing and evacuation of toxic wastes, unhealthy buildup and imbalance of various forms of physical, emotional, and mental energy. Disease permits a return to greater overall balance. Such an effect as the human fever is a good example of one type of response to disease of the system intended to bring about an eventual return to balance.

The fever is the body's way of raising its temperature to the point where destructive factors can be eliminated. Of course, if the body is too weakened, and if it has not been monitoring itself and responding to early warning signs, the fever can, on occasion, kill due to overloading an already weakened system. But if the body does respond early, wasting disease can be avoided. Appropriate balance can be returned, and the system brought back to a renewed state of health. Our most pressing problems in the next century will be the result of overpopulation and greed mixed. This results in an unhealthy situation where goods and services are not equitably distributed throughout the system, leading to a buildup of toxic waste nodes, which must be cleansed and flushed from the system.

Disease forces us to reorganize, to re-recognize ourselves, and this is true in all systems. Planetary imbalances also serve the useful adaptive purpose of forcing us to either heed the warning signs and respond properly early on, or suffer increasing disorder and turbulence as the pressure and heat increase. We must gently, gradually reorganize our systems to change the parts in ways that benefit the greater whole. To not do so is to invite disaster, disease, and war into our living systems, and to suffer in direct proportion to the degree of our failure to heed the messages the parts send out. We must maintain our awareness of how to grow without hurting ourselves.

When communication between the protective factors and the mind breaks down, disease will result whether in the planetary, cultural, or personal and cellular levels of living systems. On the individual level this happens to the body of the bereaved, divorced, or infected individuals. When their resistance to disease is weakened by instability of identity and attendant failure of communications between the brain, white blood cells and other immune factors, illness or death can result. From the global perspective a lack of communication can result in the breakdown or death of cultures, societies or even whole civilizations.

It is imperative that we keep the planetary mind and body healthy, the channels of communication between them open. We need to develop an expanded sense of our own identity in order to remain healthy and respond to the needs of the greater whole.

This requires us to look beyond the merely localized sense of self and identity, towards the greater whole, the we, the complete being of the cosmos. We must understand the vaporous nature, the tenuous quality of our existence, and unify within and without in order to cleanse and purify, to flush the toxic elements which do us so much harm. For, as Henry David Thoreau said, "when we die, what we call our self evaporates as if it were fiction."

Immunity and National Identity

As suggested in previous chapters there is a link between identity and immunity. In Ayurvedic medicine, as was noted, they are considered to be a single complex. The purpose of the immune system is to recognize and destroy anything in the body that is dangerous to itself. This is a complex process, with many degrees of subtlety, few absolutes, and a lot of free play. The immune system uses fever, initially, to destroy invaders when the phagocytes cannot consume all the disease-inducing organisms or toxic substances. But the immune system is a two-edged system. When it goes haywire, it can even destroy the host body, as it is unable to distinguish between that which is part of the body and that which is not. When this happens, systemic breakdown occurs and destroys all else, in order to quell the infection.

On the national and planetary scale we have, by analogy, immune systems in the form of military forces, arsenals of weaponry, deadly biological agents, and nuclear missiles. The purpose of these units is to destroy anything which attempts to invade a culture system, or trespass national boundaries. Whatever crosses the borders by which the nation identifies itself will be captured. If it cannot be absorbed, it is destroyed. Any inassimilable agent from another system is looked upon as threatening, dangerous, as infectious, for it represents an alternate frame of reference that is perceived as antagonistic to the culture. The most obvious example is that of America and Russia during the Cold War. More recent examples can be seen in the variety of regional, ethnic, and religious conflicts across the globe.

All across the planet the systems by which cultures protect their selves are now in need of alteration, for we live in a coming age of fusion, integration, and increasingly universal availability of information. If we do not willingly undergo gradual interconnection, and come to recognize that all human life—in fact, all existence on this planet—is joined in a common process of adaptation and survival, we will find ourselves excluded from life. We will continue to be hopelessly divided, and eventually become inoperative. Our planetary immune systems could conceivably destroy the whole of humanity.

There are only eight or nine nuclear nations, and these are making treaties to control the proliferation of weapons. But smaller nations, terrorist cells, and madmen are seeking to obtain such devices of mass destruction in order to blackmail those around them. Such as these could be wild cards that might be able to commit actions of the most destructive sort.

Fission is the basis for these most potent defenses. Its explosive potentials have proven to be the most destructive force ever unleashed.

Such forces have their valuable side though, for they force us to see that in order to join in a more lasting union, to prevent mutual self-destruction, a political system must reduce resistance to others, and allow its boundaries more permeability.

On the other hand, the fusion process gives off energy in the form of heat and light, through the unification of nuclei. The resulting new element has some characteristics of both of the originals, but is unlike either. When the cores fuse, a new identity is formed that allows reformation rather than disintegration, and which gives off useful energy in the joining. This is not only a nuclear process, but also a cultural and national one.

The earth is very flexible and strong. But human civilization and its environments are quite fragile. We cannot actually destroy a planet, but we can easily destroy ourselves. Our fission-based defenses can still go haywire if humanity proves to be too dangerous to the planetary mind and body. Yet, the fusion process is inevitable. Scientists have almost succeeded in accomplishing this miraculous feat in the physical realm. It is up to all of us to bring it about in the human sphere.

The first step in this process is to shift gradually over the next few decades to a hydrogen-based fuel economy. Thus the power of oil producing nations to hold the rest of the world hostage to their energy addiction will be minimized or eliminated. Sun and air and water are far superior to underground fluids and gases as sources of power.

Through the planetary telecommunications networks all our human systems are gradually being connected. The diverse elements of human consciousness are being fused instead of refused. A time is coming when we might all realize and accept our mutual humanity. We might become truly intelligent, cooperative, and able to withstand the stress of diversity and ambiguity without self-destructing. We are now able to communicate with a citizen of Russia, Iraq, North Korea, or China via direct computer links.

Already transnational data flows transcend national boundaries and borders. Our sense of identity in the developed world is already becoming progressively more international, especially as the Internet, the so-called "Information Superhighway" (which is actually more like the wagon trails of the nineteenth century than it is like our modern interstate highways) develops and gradually shapes and defines the unexplored electronic continent of the cyber-sphere. Some insular nations are so fearful of "globalization" that they are limiting or preventing their population access to the system.

When the process of global fusion and reunion is one day complete, we shall be able to develop a healthy planetary identity. We will permanently overcome, through the union of all peoples into a singular functioning system, the threats of nuclear fission, environmental degradation, and self-destruction.

Information Viruses

Information viruses are, by analogy, pathological forms of mental activity that are transmitted generationally through the familial and social communications systems, and expressed as degenerative, degrading behaviors such as domestic violence, drug abuse, and other forms of destructive action. Biological viruses are usually pathological forms of biota that replicate uncontrollably and bear only an incomplete message (in this case in the form of RNA without its complement DNA). These viruses lead the organism into a debilitating immune response, or the stimulation of other systems of excessive heat generation (fever) and loss, or static; then we know that such forms of pathology can in fact cause what we describe as the symptoms of illness, or of a change of state in the physical systems: Death.

Likewise there are the recently developed computer viruses, which are, as per their analogous description, debilitating forms of information that invade a processing system and cause it to break down—to change states as they descend into chaos. In this case, the virus is in the form of a sort of "electronic noise" that selectively disrupts critical memory links and renders the information processing system inoperative.

The effects of some types of viral invasion, in the Middle Ages and before, were attributed to the presence of ghosts or spirits that were in possession of the systemic body and rendered it uncontrollable. There were developed specific spoken forms of information—exorcism—to combat and neutralize these mental pathological messages, before antiviral agents for the physical system were developed, beginning in Colonial times. Now we have vaccines against both biological and computer viruses.

Methods of retrieval and reformation of computer memory damaged by viruses have been developed. And we can even look at psychology as a crude attempt to develop an antiviral mental technology. Using trans-active communications process and interactive biochemical and neuro-chemical alterations of neural pathways, psychologists attempt to restore balance to systems exposed to, and disrupted by virulent psychological messages.

Attempts to render information viruses inactive or unable to repli-cate and spread are being made even today. We seek to eliminate domestic violence, drug addiction, and other pathological conditions wrought by these incomplete forms of information. Ancient philoso-phers such as Socrates thought of people as inherently good, and that they would act against the greater good only out of ignorance—a lack of complete, coherent information.

It must be remembered that some information viruses can thus be transmitted through the medium of language. They may enter the mind in the process of conditioning in early childhood in the home and by the educational system later. They may be imprinted on the mind in a latent form to be activated by later conditions such as stress, or can remain in the system after behaviors and perceptions have been altered in such a way as to suggest their demise. However, in fact they will arise once new pathways to expression are found.

Any type of healing is thus an attempt to find information that neutralizes the incomplete, debilitating, virulent forms of understand-ing—the "sensory delusions"—that wreak havoc in communications systems and make them unhealthy and unable to operate at their opti-mum.

Many older cultures have ritual, ceremony, myth, and other forms of normative expression that keep information viruses in check, or at least at a minimum. When a culture is lacking in such normative forms, pathological conditions can proliferate, to the point even of disabling the culture over time. American culture in particular has little in the way of coherent traditions that can be drawn upon to lessen violence and fill out the gaps in our incomplete understanding of ourselves and world around us. Thus the culture is poised forever on the edge of chaos, and violence, criminal activity, and destructive behavior proliferate.

In our day we must develop forms of communication that are so coherent that an "infected" party cannot resist them. Such forms alter perceptions and thus behavior in a way that is benevolent and beneficent. Integrative knowledge operates by altering neural pathways and actions in profound and dramatic ways. Nobody can resist its own best hope unless it is prepared to die. No one wants to act against their own and others' best interests except out of ignorance.

Those with the greatest pathology will resist neutralization of their information viruses, such as Colonial minister Cotton Mather, who resisted the use of inoculation for Pilgrim colonists. This resulted in many deaths, until Benjamin Franklin saw the sense of it. Inoculation with healthy information is likewise rendered difficult at times due to personal or social resistance.

We can all see that planetary aberrations resulting from information viruses are unconstructive and deadly. We find it difficult to understand and accept that wars, pollution, and exploitation of the poor are manifestations of information pathogens. Such negative manifestations of human potentials are often the only signs that breakdown is imminent as population reaches its maximal threshold.

We are the only form of life and mind that has managed to evolve to the point where we have the capacity to choose our future state. When we are all able to live within the earth together, to be healed of our common diseases as a race, we will then join in the process of creation as co-creators, free of dis-ease that devours the weak, and weakens the strong. Then we will be imbued with the light that emanates from the source of life itself, attain lasting health and well-being, and be at peace in our planetary minds.

Social Superconductivity

Patterns of thought, or ideas both good and bad, often take root in and proliferate in the social medium. When organized in a good way, they can be used to inoculate the information system against the deleterious effects of pathogenic elements that often make their way through the population virtually without resistance. There are certain patterns of energy in formation that are so universally meaningful that they even give rise to similar sounds in many languages (such as the words for mother and father around the world), and they are desirable to hear to the point that they have been seen as "food for the soul."

In other times and places such ideas were recorded as chants, mantras, incantations, invocations, prayers, and hymns, and acted out as ceremony, ritual, and mythic dramas. These expressions of the community are part of their way of life. To live in this way created a shared contemplative state governed from within. The resistance between bodies was in this way rectified, impedance was minimized, and all the members of the group brought closer together by their lack of resistance to the health-inducing information.

Superconductivity is the patterned movement of electronic currents through solids without resistance. This means no heat buildup or loss, and a corresponding rise in the speed the currents of energy can move. There is a concurrent rise in the number of operations that can be handled per second per circuit or network.

Social superconductivity is the social application and extension of the idea of waves of energy in formation moving without resistance through many human beings at the same time—moving in such a way as to not generate static or distortions in communications that can give rise to misunderstanding, disagreement, conflict, violence, or other flare-ups resulting from excessive tension and dissonance within the system.

Some complexes of thought can take vast populations by storm: the divine rights of kings, humanism, consumerism, democracy, individualism, communism, Islam, Christianity, etc. They spread into every land and take on unique forms depending on how the people among whom they arise make use of them. Some virulent forms, such as Nazism, Stalinism, and terrorism have found fertile ground among confused populations weakened by the state of their constitution, just as diseases spread among the concentrated urban populations of the Middle Ages which were so taken with the overwhelming devastation of the plague.

The works of great writers who accurately describe human nature are imbued with a virtual magnetism or gravity that draws readers across the ages together in mutual consideration of the human condition. Such words have great attraction because they are written with great love, and as such they are irresistible. Their verbal and literary formulas, every bit as complex in their overtones as orchestral symphonies, every bit as appealing to the feelings and thoughts as glorious sunsets, are representative of our shared experience across thousands of years. The body of their works is one of the finest gifts bestowed by nature upon any person within a population. Such voices become the voices of the community, and what such a one says emerges from the shared soul of the group, to be shared by all of humanity.

In the most complex parts of our self-awareness we are drawn to absorb and consider those ideas that appeal universally to the needs of the individual and society. When such ideas arise, though they may take thousands of years to become clear and a part of the collective memory, or even hundreds of generations, they are the source of our myths, of mystery, identity and worldviews. They burn through the convolutions of the planetary mind as a storm, or as a healing flame.

From bones under the ground to satellites far out in space, the memories of human beings are stored, living information. They provide guidance against chaos and breakdown, beacons to shine into our collective past and out among the other planets. Our collective memory remains forever for us to discover. Rolling through the endlessness of space, across the fiber optic and satellite networks, it signals at light speed the thoughts of a world exploding in immense conflagrations. Thus go those forms of organized energy that meet no resistance. They join us all in a singular identity, its core as impervious to harm as titanium.

With our electromagnetic telecommunications we broadcast a sphere of radiation one hundred light years across from our world. It is unimpeded as it moves through the cosmos to everywhere at once, forever. This halo of electromagnetic information is full of the energy in formation of the human imagination in all its diversity and beauty. This is a wondrous thing we do, and we do it collectively, effortlessly, and endlessly.

To surrender our resistance to the nameless quality that sustains life and self-awareness is the beginning of healing. It is the opening up to the kind of integrated identification with the communal, global, and universal mind that brings wholeness, peace, and sustenance to all.

As we make our personal, community, national, ethnic and religious barriers more permeable to the messages from far away that fill the very atmosphere around us and lift us outward light years in every direction, we become more unified and peaceful. The process of globalization spreads as we, as a world, broaden our experience of the many aspects of our shared lives which were previously unknown from one people to another. Now we are being gradually inoculated with meaningful energy in formation that tells us of our common inheritance and plight. With social superconductivity increasingly lowering the resistance between nations and peoples internationally, a peaceful, unitary and diverse mindfulness, and global well-being, can spread at an optimum rate beneficial to as many as possible.

Who can resist such a benevolent conception? The earth lives in us, and we live in it. The less resistance the mind has to new information the more easily it can adapt to rapidly changing conditions. Change takes place as new ideas spread and are adopted. The mind is enriched. New thoughts are conducted through society, weightless and digital. They move through the networks without resistance, and we are renewed, healed, and able to see new ways in which we can come to be unified, peaceful, and prosperous as a species.

Convolutions of the Planetary Mind

As the fetal brain develops, convolutions appear. These folds in the cortex increase its surface area by many times as they differentiate out from the immature cells. They specialize as they develop. There is an increase in the richness and lushness of the energy processing system. The electrical signal the cells send and receive occurs in patterns, and these form our thoughts. Self-consciousness emerges from our thinking processes, from the complex organism that provides the basis of our being. The mind increases its network of interconnections and improves the resolution and clarity of thought processes in developing greater complexity. More connections, more awareness! The connective network becomes entrenched and expands through the experience of interacting with the environment—more interactions, more interconnections as the surface area increases.

Likewise, the many convolutions of the planetary surface act as a means whereby more solar radiation can be collected, stored, transformed and utilized. Through processes of physical transformation, photons activate electrons—the electromagnetic effect coupled with Brownian motion—which gather around localized atomic nuclear forms to create the molecular and chemical substances that keep the earth a living, active and dynamic body spinning and circling through the heavens.

Whether through plants, animals, or technological devices, our great ability as human beings is to project our thoughts into the material substrata of the natural environment through means embedded in language. The tools and forms are transmitted from one generation to the next through cultural conditioning. We pass on the information to others, which allows humans to increase their degree of interconnection. The more people who are connected and understand one another, the richer the convolutions of the planetary mind become. Humans develop the ability to manufacture technologies that increase the ability of the planet as a whole, and humans in particular, to harness the solar sources more efficiently for the benefit of all.

The language we share is at the root of our understanding of ourselves, of others and of the world around us. The greater the number of connections between people, the greater the level of shared awareness. From that shared awareness we develop the most efficient means of interacting with the environment to extract our energy and other needs.

A solar- and hydrogen-based energy economy would answer many problems and current imbalances caused by the use of carbon-based fuels. The use of hydrocarbon-based products—from wood, to coal, to oil—which burn dirty and decay slowly, causes problems in the environment leading to long-term ecological degradation and accumulation of toxic wastes in the natural world. The more of the sun's energy we can harness, the greater our ability to continue our growth. The more efficiently and effectively we can use our resources, and the more equitable and equalized our sharing and exchange systems, the less our internal tensions and conflicts. The greater our degree of environmental conservatism as relates to energy extraction and use, the more people we can support.

We will meet our maximum growth potential somewhere between ten billion and twenty billion people, part way into the new century. We will then most probably experience a return to balance. This could take the form of a massive die-off of our excess numbers, and a great sobering up of the global population as the results of uncontrolled growth, unregulated, destructive, unsustainable lifestyles, and insensitive development policies centered on short-term growth reach their climax. By the time this inevitable rebalancing of the human ecological system occurs, we will hopefully have learned ways to sustain our kind for the long term through both locally centered, but globally inclusive energy distribution, sharing, and use. The lesson will be learned, easy or hard. The less desirable form of nature's response is to simply end human existence. We've not been around that long, and the world will continue without humanity, long after we've destroyed ourselves or gone extinct.

The more convolutions we have, the greater our potentials for intelligence and creativity due to interconnectivity, and the greater our ability to harvest, store, and use the energy of the sun. Our choices at the end of the twentieth century have determined the likely outcomes of the human experience in the twenty-first century. On a planetary scale resolution of the energy problem is being sought through those systems that communicate our natural interdependence. We express our level of development by how far away we have come from use of the fossil fueled fire as a means of controlling nature, and violence as a means of ordering our societies. We have increased our productive capacities, improved the distribution of goods and services—albeit the greed and profit motives in the current political and corporate systems makes this process slug-gish—and begun the process of extending the fiber optic networks into every nook and cranny of the globe.

We really are an amazing event, we human beings. Against all odds we act as the medium for the continuing growth of the planetary mind, and the development and spread of intelligence and consciousness throughout the world.

The Fruiting Planet

Teilhard de Chardin suggested that one day the earth will be com-pletely covered in a living network of consciousness he called the "noosphere." He compared this to the mycelial mat of mushrooms. We see various types of mushroom in our fields and relish the taste in certain cases, or we can pick some and prepare them for use in mind alteration. In other instances they can cause death where care is not exercised. The mat, from which the fruit blossoms, grows beneath the ground and is unseen most of the time.

By analogy the atmosphere we live in is similar to the moist recesses of grassy pastures where the mushrooms grow. And we are, according to Chardin, the medium of growth for the planetary mind and global consciousness. We project our extensions of earthly forms beyond the narrow folds of the photo emulsion in which we grow. The telecommunications network provides the connectivity, and such devices as planes, rockets, spacecraft, and the Voyager and Pioneer probes are "fruits" every bit as much as mushrooms.

We express our magical abilities by projecting and impressing the patterns originating in our own minds onto the substantial forms of the materials we live among. The fruits of our knowledge and labor are the basis for the many civilizations that have developed across the world over the ages, and the artifacts that are the remnants of our living history. We are the flowers, and what we make is the fruit when we are fertilized with inspirations that erupt from the collective mind through individuals and groups. We are inspired and nourished to bring about constructive changes and improve life for all as we gradually grow. We then send the seeds of our growth across the interstellar medium in hopes that they might one day find, and take root in, another hospitable planet.

So Chardin was correct, and the fiber optic web which we are currently wrapping around the whole planet is the requisite element of the system, and the foundation for the emerging global consciousness. Many layers of nutriment have been laid down to fertilize our growth in the form of layers of past civilizations that leave their remains for our consideration. We encounter therein the forms of knowledge which have been developed to act as inspiration to those here and yet to come, which will stimulate and motivate them to express potentials for consciousness in their next form.

The planet is fruiting in silicon, gold, platinum, and other rare and precious alloys that are used in creating our space vehicles and communications systems. These are amazing fruits. These are the expressions of a living mind, a mind that we contain, and are contained by, which is operating throughout creation, and the cosmos. It is operating in marvelous and wondrous ways to which we can pay only our deepest reverence and respect, however it is named.

That mind is both source and receiver of the messages we as a human information-processing network generate. The delight we feel in our creative accomplishments can only be the shadow of what the systems of being throughout creation experience when stars are born, and when lifeless planets start singing in their suns of the systems of our shared being.

Our fruiting planet is on fire with words that live. We exist in a fiery blaze of informational media that keeps us warm and excited. The words we live by are part of us, as we are part of them. As long as the words live in us and are the basis for what we share, then we are still fertile with the possibility of growth and continued adaptation.

The Living Word Now

There are no truly original thoughts. All possible ideas exist in potential. An individual mind must develop in such a way as to be able to host, hold, or conceive of ever more complex forms of thought, which call upon an ever-increasing portion of the brain's potential abilities. The more advanced and complex the thought forms, the less effort, and hence less resistance occurs in the system.

Functionally and structurally the brain exists as a sort of organic hardware, or "wetware" as some call it. Input from birth, from innate genetic traits, from the surrounding environment—all act as software, or programming. This programming is the unique synthesis of sensory information, perceptual recognition, and neurolinguistic memory of our common organismic and biosocial historical inheritance and individual experience. It is the basis for the mind, or personality; it is at the very core of the identity of the person.

Our sensory modalities are multiple, our thought processes multiplex, our emotional chemistry energetic, and our physical bodies but passing mediums for a greater state of being beyond the individual. We are each a matrix of energy within which a vast and complex biological and cellular physical body grows, develops, and is eventually sloughed off, liberating the original energy to return to its source.

At any given moment, all around the world, countless minds and bodies are generating and monitoring an endless variety of thoughts. Yet all the purely verbal forms of thought are the voice within, the internalized aspect of self-expression, functionally supported by complex networks of helical, closed-loop, feedback-monitoring circuits. These circuits are composed of a limited (less than sixty in most cases) number of units of neuronal activity designated to represent the phonemic units of speech. As such, thought forms exist apart from language, yet the form of the language in which they are expressed tends to expand or limit their potential to become manifest in the various forms of language, math, music, science or technology, etc.

Symbolic, meaningful patterns of firing exist in the brain in a sort of living form. It is only when they become manifest as written, recorded, externalized forms that they solidify and become static, dead, no longer active within a living system. The Living Word is transformed into localized information. Without the word that lives in man, that delights in taking up residence in highly developed minds, there could be no communication, no awareness beyond the bounds of one's instincts as mediated by their personal and communal experience. With the understanding of the Living Word in our lives we become sorcerers, wizards, seers, shamans, artists, scientists and other sorts of magical beings.

The ability to take electrochemical and neuronal forms and translate them into signals that become plans, actions, and finally externalized forms of creation from within the self, is nothing short of amazing, magical, perhaps even miraculous. We are so used to it now that we often forget that it is so, take it for granted, and become powerless rather than empowered by its influence. In its ideal form the Living Word dissolves all boundaries between races, nations, and peoples, brings about a planetary resolution and global understanding. Such is the hope that myths are formed of, that gives messiahs life and death, that drives us onward towards the uncertain and unknown.

The Living Word is the means by which creation is made manifest in humankind. Nearly all that exists around us, that we have created, started out as a thought in someone's head. The thought, or pattern of brain cells firing, was then transformed into the Living Word and the process of manifestation begun. It lives above and beyond individuals, yet takes the form each individual desires. Dream, write them down, act on them, and your desires will take on form in direct proportion to the quantity and quality of focus and intent the action takes. The degree of awareness and self-development, and the overall effort invested in the living process of giving life and form to our thoughts and words is central to the development of civilization.

Highly advanced thoughts alight like stray birds in many minds at once. The number of hours humanity invests in the manifesting of these higher thoughts determines the shape and nature of our cultures. Great forms of thought become reality because literally millions of hours are spent (in both mental and, in our day, computer time) finding ways to manifest them. Need, necessity, profit, love—all are motives for the creative act. The way the Living Word takes form in man, and the forms made of it, can be either creative or destructive. Systems theory indicates that there be an equal measure of potential for planetary thoughts built into each thing.

In order for harmony to be approached on anything near a planetary scale, common goals must be arrived at by humanity. The only goal we have true need of bringing about is peace within ourselves, our families, our communities, and our nations: The end of war can be the beginning of a truly collective consciousness. The resources of the peoples of the world, which have been forged into weapons, into disintegrating consumer products of marginal value, must be returned to them. Providing basic necessities to every person might enable more to take self-responsibility, provide for their own family as well as other members of the local community. Then each person can live a life in which the further development of consciousness is possible. It is not possible to develop a properly unified consciousness without basic necessities.

This is a multi-faceted goal, pursued by poets and politicians, by doctors and lawyers, by sensitive, thinking peoples everywhere. This is especially true in the well-off nations, who must bear the burden of upheaval due to changes that are inevitable if peace is to come. Due to the advent of modern telecommunications, especially the recent expansion in the uses of fiber optics technology—which would ultimately put everyone in touch everywhere instantaneously, at light-speed—the possibility of a collective consciousness is imminent. But such nations as are wealthy and create the means for world alteration will have to undergo the most drastic changes in lifestyle and perception of themselves and others. We can have individuals, communities, and nations, but not if they are going to form conflicting entities and institutions.

This is not a query or supposition, no theory or prognostication. We must seek peace, encourage continuing planetary interconnectedness, freedom and dignity for all humans and ways of life. Nobody wants to be subjected to unwilling death or forced to adhere to the illusions of temporality inherent in our fragmented world views. All sane peoples wish to avoid atomic conflagration and environmental exhaustion and have a future. Either harmony will be brought about by the spread of understanding wrought by the Living Word as it has moved among mankind these many thousands of years, or our civilizations as they exist will die. Should that occur, it will take ages to return the world to balance, with no guarantees that mankind would be able to continue for long in a revised world.

The Living Word is the beginning of life, god, love, culture, and creativity. For humanity would be nothing without it but animals driven by instinct, at worst, or ignorant, distant, violent, tribal or politically institutionalized savages at best, bent only on their own gratification and the exploitation of the weak and weaponless.

We are speaking here of a planetary revolution that may take several hundred, or even a few thousand years to bring about. It cannot be accomplished without turmoil, pain, and suffering on the part of many. It cannot come about except we be willing to hope, to give, and to work for the good of all. Only through communication can such changes be wrought. Only by intercultural exchange and understanding can we come to appreciate our diversity, our differences, what we share, and what is thus at stake for the greater whole.

Through science, art, and technology all peoples have been advanced, or given the potential for advancement. It is true that natural disaster, or unforeseen events could stop us in our course, but barring such disaster, of natural or man-made variety, we can bring about a better world for our children. Is this not what we all desire after our basic needs are fulfilled? After all, what can we do but prepare for the coming generations? All peoples must approach such questions.

Localized beliefs are not the source of understanding. The only common faith we can share is based on breathing and being alive and warm. We must approach cooperation and tolerance in spite of our differences and the ambiguity and uncertainty that is generated thereby. We must promote understanding and communication, and be willing to "under-react" to offense, be it real or imagined. We must further be willing to quickly take steps to prevent the injury or exploitation of local peoples and resources as a unified civilization. We must finally be intent on the discouragement of all who would disrupt the common good.

As a poet, writer, and teacher I have sought to spread the self-evident doctrine of planetary unity. As a Native American I have worked to preserve the culture and dignity of all persons, in order to preserve what we can that is of value, and to make whatever degree of assimilation is necessary, and a certain loss of local history, more bearable. The more peoples there are, the more ways of life they represent, and the greater our capacity as a race to adapt to new circumstances, whether they originate in nature, or emerge from our humanity.

These are the things I have studied and will continue to convey to all. On whatever scale life directs we must act to manifest a hopeful, realistic future for our children, and for everyone eventually. We must all contribute in whatever small or large way we can, must realize our potential as human beings in order that all might benefit, and must devote ourselves to the Living Word, which is the heart of all understanding.

Perhaps one can only dream in the night, sing in the dark, and hope for the best, doing whatever their better judgment says is necessary. One must use the Living Word to create the next form of our civilization and world, however possible. Even if one only finds peace within, another step towards the great goal is achieved. To then give it to others is the highest form of service, the most creative and gratifying political action possible. Great souls live for this service. All others serve life as they can. And this must be enough for now.

III

The Unfinished Universe

WHAT'S IN A WORD? Words appear to have a life of their own. Still, no one knows where it all began, or why. In an unpredictable world, among an improbable species, where little is for certain, speech communication is most certainly a fortunate accident. One communications writer goes so far as to say, "Speech is civilization itself." Recent studies indicate that over time areas of the brain devoted to visual processing were rewired in order to give us the ability to speak.

Yet, when we speak, we don't really know just exactly what it is that we are sending to each other, and for that matter, across the world to peoples of other lands, and even out into space and across the vast interstellar distances where our radio and television signals ride the waves of space-time—to who knows where? What is meaning? You cannot grab hold of it, yet you can apprehend and grasp it. It has no mass, yet can carry a lot of weight. It has no density, yet words have some sort of gravity.

You cannot see it, but you know what I mean as you experience what I write or speak. No one has yet come to define meaning clearly, and I will not presume to do so here. Syntax and semantics have been created to help us understand the rules that govern the processes of its creation and transmission. But, we need a way of talking about it, as a convenience. And since exactness is not the goal, but metaphor and adventure, and since all of our human descriptions are mere approximations and analogies, I will suggest what meaning means to me.

The universe is made up of energy. The known frequencies of electromagnetism are very broad, and our senses can perceive only a very narrow bandwidth. But with the aid of devices we have invented, we can see beyond sight, sense light in darkness, and gain awareness of the invisible.

Our senses are composed in such a way that we can discern patterns in our surroundings. The light of the sun is diffuse, a random glowing, but we sense to the core of our beings the cycles of day and night. Our circadian rhythms are so powerful that a simple change of time zones can throw our whole metabolism off for days. The seasons, the weather patterns, the ebb and flow of tides, the rise and fall of animal and plant life around us, and perhaps most important, the rise and fall of consciousness within, give evidence to the imprint made upon us by the patterns we see as life and death.

Such patterns are the stuff upon which our earliest myths are based, with which they deal, and the expressions of those myths in the form of art. The more static forms of religions, philosophies, and sciences are the basis for our behavior towards one another and the environment. But what must be most evident and best remembered is in the form of stories in words, movements in ancient dances, the harmonic qualities of musical accompaniment.

So, it is my idea that what we human beings sense as being meaningful is patterned, ordered, cyclic forms of energy. Here is the equation I use: Meaning is energy in formation. Energy that is not information is meaning-less. The patterns of language represent the patterns of activity within and around us, and are stored in our minds as energy that is in formation and therefore meaningful. And it is in the formations of the group language, the culture, the civilization that we have stored the meaningful patterns of life to give to coming generations.

The psychologist Alfred Adler said, "the life of the soul is in the community." The word comm-unity means exactly that, communications unity. So, the life of the community is in the word. And the energy of the word is in-formation. Random sounds are experienced as noise, or static, in our information systems, and such noise, in fact, distorts the transmission of messages. We need patterned, orderly, clear signals and sounds to communicate. These sounds take the form of the many languages of the peoples of the world. And the variation of themes and content is vast, even though all share the basics of life. Thus we return to the initial question: what's in a word?

In order to answer it, we must first define what a word is. Words are not things. Nor do words actually describe things. Words are patterns of sound that we use to correspond to patterns of activity in our own brains. They are "cognitive tags" used to organize our internal activities. It may have been millions of years ago when human beings first began to use sounds to describe mental activity, the brain's responses to the combined input of the senses. As shared language developed a unique pattern of knowledge and activity evolved, which we often describe with the inexact term of "culture," or the somewhat better word "community."

As we named what we experienced, what we saw took on meaning, our perception of the world was enlarged, and our brains, in response, developed new ways of ordering input, transmitting signals to others, and interacting with the environment. A modern conception called the "Law of Linguistic Relativity" says that, when language is altered, so are perceptions, and by extension so are the objects of perception. And it is these shared perceptions, and the words used to represent them, that form the basis of community, culture, and civilization. These, in turn, are what give meaning, shape, order, and form to our experiences.

With our words we attempt to create an integrated, coherent picture of the world as we experience it. The more accurate and adequate the descriptions we create, the better able we are to regulate and organize our environments in such a way as to support our group life, and to thus nourish our identity and our souls. So words are signals that represent the activity of our brains in response to experience. And the order, the pattern of these signals, the energy in formation of language is a carrier of meaning, and the basis for comm-unity.

What we believe is what we see. The conditioned responses to our world begin to shape us at conception, and are continually re-informed through the agency of language. We are informed of our identity through words, which represent how we order the group, the environment, the world, and the universe we exist in. But our descriptions are not, and cannot ever be complete, for our senses are only partial, our perceptions limited, and what actually exists is beyond us, beyond our ability to conceive and speak of. Thus the universe is never complete; it forever remains unfinished. And human life, unpredictable, uncertain, improbable, is thus never finished either.

Though the number of choices we can describe is perhaps limited, which choices we actually make never set the possibilities in stone. The broader, more comprehensive our view of the world, and the language we use to describe it, the more meaningful our lives will be, the more completely we will feel the experience of life.

It has been the occupation of creative minds throughout human history to seek to more clearly understand the mystery, magic, and power of words, for within them lies our capacity for civilization, order, and understanding. The diverse forms of civilization across our planet are testament to the variety of choices possible, and available to us.

And now a new environment is emerging, our consciousness is expanding at an incredible rate as the richness of our interconnectivity increases through the global telecommunications media. A few basic language systems are becoming universal. Both spoken English, and binary digital encoding, are necessary for commerce and computers throughout the civilized world. These languages are the carriers of the meanings that are operative in much of the collective mind as it extends itself in every direction seeking self-awareness and an increased capacity to regulate and organize itself in ever more orderly, complex, and efficient ways.

We must each take responsibility for ourselves as individuals, groups, and as a species. It is imperative that we do everything in our power to aid the earth as it develops a mind of its own and a comprehensive language with which to communicate with itself through us. Any living system must do this if it is to maintain a dynamic steady state of equilibrium and continued growth. Our populations are expanding so fast, technology is proliferating so rapidly, that whether we like it or not we must prepare for major changes in our world within the next three generations.

All systems, previous to undergoing a change of state, give off noise, static, or other disorderly forms of energy—for cells it is heat, for cultures it is conflict, for environments it is pollution—which attend the turbulent phases of initial transformation. The world is a noisy place, and we must somehow find the meaning in it. And it is through words, communication, and language that we can do so. We are not finished yet.

A living system is an open, forever unfinished system, and therefore able to adapt, whether it is a cell, a culture, a planet, a solar system, a galaxy, or a person like you or me. And as long as we are alive, words are alive, and in that is our greatest hope and strength.

The Incredible Accident of Being

We shouldn't be here. We are not predictable or likely. Our genetic lines, whose potentials arose out of the beginning of the universe, emerged on earth in the Cambrian explosion. Any of an incalculable number of conditions could have existed at any given juncture in our evolutionary process which would have fractured our line, weakened our constitution, fragmented our being and consigned us to the evolutionary scrap heap, not selected, dead, a dark whisper in the empty halls of non-being.

In our own human brains, the marvelous junctions between neurons quite possibly outnumber the stars, and mirror the complexion and complexity of the physical cosmos in a startling array of magnificent constellations we view as our thoughts. Mathematicians suggest that our cosmos may indeed be only one of zillions in an interconnected cosmos. Just as with human neuronal junctions, so it is with the evolutionary junctions. They are points of rise and fall upon which we stumble or arise into the multiple beings which form the biological mass of the planet.

The planet does not need to imagine us humans, nor are we crucial as functionaries, or as a means of developing earthly self-conception in a planetary mind. Any of a multitude of other possible forms would serve as well. But here we are, an incredible accident of being, one of the lucky bunches of cells that managed to survive among the multitudes that have ceased to be. Still, the planet can imagine itself through us and, due to our activity, see itself, hear itself, and extend its perceptions in fruiting bodies of precious metals and silicon beyond our solar system towards the galactic heart, the black hole singularity from which our light emerges to create the multi-layered intelligence of which we alone seem to be the projectors.

It is our wonder and curiosity that are the marvel of our beings, and that we can, alone among all species, capture the constellations of thought in symbols and actions. We alone can project these patterns of energy in formation into the material substrata we are embedded within. We reorganize the organic and inorganic matrices to which we are bound into the myriad forms of culture, technology, society, and civilization on a global scale.

It is in this regard I am willing to suggest that the world we have made for ourselves can be, by analogy, said to compose a vast shared hallucination that has taken on material form through the human energy systems. We are the result of a universe dreaming it exists, and, as we look out on creation, we can see nothing more or less than ourselves, than a cosmos that exists for us, because of us, and as a result of us.

It is an accident that we can consider our mortality and tenure as mere temporal functionaries in the bounded chaos that we are part of. We realize at the furthest extent of our being that we, like all organic forms, are not eternal, while at the same time being aware that the energy of which we are made lasts forever. We also know that there will yet one day be a world without people, a planet free of human beings, yet what we are made of cannot be created or destroyed, only transformed.

It has been suggested that there is emerging, out of all of this human activity, a cognitive planet. Such a living globe will be able to engage in the processes of self-awareness and project its nature into the cosmos in a possibly futile search for someone else, another sentient world perhaps, to talk to. Another interesting suggestion is that we might well be creating our own replacement as carbon-ring based intelligence sparks the gap and leaps into the silicon matrix. There it will be impervious to radiation, free of dependence on the carbon and oxygen cycles that make organic life so fragile and subject to decay and extinction.

As with all analogies we are dealing here with possibility, skirting the edge of theology, extending science into the human being, and recomposing the arts to somehow make the bold attempt to more adequately define human experience. We are creating sets of ideas that expand our awareness rather than imprison it in the bonds of that uncreative imagining that limits our being and confines our consciousness within the walled edifices of current conceptions—conceptions that limit us to wondering just what kind of incredible accident we are, and how we somehow remain alive in the midst of this accident.

We exist in direct defiance of probability, and there is no theory that can describe or contain the immeasurable and vast wonderment a child feels, which creates in us a susceptible tenderness and openness to alternative viewpoints and realities. It makes us vulnerable to others in such a way as to elevate our mere reproductive activity into the mythic realms of love. It joins us in families, communities, cultures and civilization regardless of our differences. It is awareness flowering in the infinite associations possible between all the things that give life a depth and meaning it may take centuries to embody fully in language and literature.

Entropy should have taken us long ago into the pit of extinction, rather than to the temporal peaks of our emergent global civilization. But we human beings are a scruffy lot and continue to find ways to harvest, store, and utilize solar energy in ever more amazing, sometimes dangerous ways. This keeps us growing and vital, but it also threatens our existence. We must go with care and concern if we are to continue to defeat extinction and the cold lifelessness of non-being. We have no choice but to accept all possibility, including that we are unnecessary and expendable. The earth does not forget or die as easily as we. Yet, as accidents go, we have lasted an incredibly long time. We will hopefully continue to last for a long time to come.

In our memories and reflections we can envision that untouchable power which gives us life and holds the cells together. For this we have no better word than love. It is this love that contains life and death. It drives the celestial process and systems we can see in our own conception, growth, structure, and developmental activity. This love guarantees nothing, and the life it confers upon us and imbues us with is neither meaningful in and of itself nor lasting.

This love is the light of life as it is reflected through our physical beings and immaterial natures. We can neither resist nor capture this power with our mundane science. We cannot extol completely its virtues with our pale poetry, nor describe with any degree of certainty its complete message with our fragmented religions. But we can take part in it for its own sake, this perpetual crash from which our civilization precipitates. We may be but an accident, but this only makes the marvel of our being here the more wondrous and incredible.

The Meaning of Magic

We humans are a strange lot. We are a unique species in a very specific way. We are the only organisms in the world that can generate patterns of activity within our brains and superimpose them on the environmental substrata. The patterns of our thoughts precipitate out and become the material and technological culture with which we are surrounded. Socio-biologists, like E.O. Wilson, in *The Selfish Gene*, have put forth the controversial idea that the genes created the body to preserve their own integrity and make it possible to transfer the information they contain in perpetuity. If this is so, then we have created the social body and its material form to protect the integrity of our collective knowledge as embodied in our human cultures so as to make it possible to hand it on from generation to generation. How do we do this?

One night I had a dream that I was carving a rock into the form of a bird. When I awoke, I saw in my mind a completed piece of sculpture in stone. In my work area I had a piece of raw stone, a beautiful chunk of deep red catlanite. This iron and sandstone rock is called "pipe stone" among American Indian peoples. But this piece was too small to make into a traditional pipe so I just kept it, knowing that it contained the shape of something which I had been waiting to work with. So, that morning I began working the dream into that piece of stone with full intensity. Nine hours later the pattern I had envisioned within my mind stood before me completed. How amazing!

Now, let us extend this instance to its maximum dimensions. Look around you. See all the objects that surround you. Now, just think; everything you see that mankind has made existed within someone's head before it came to have a material form! The transference of waves of electro-chemical activity in our brains into what, by analogy, are standing wave fronts held in suspension in the denser materials of stone, wood, metal, plastic, etc., is a phenomenon worthy of our notice. We take it for granted. It is so common we are surrounded by it. But what does it suggest? What is the meaning of this?

Originally human beings were mere gatherers of seeds, nuts, fruits, and other foods. But somewhere in our dim past the human mind envisioned the digging stick, the sharp blade and the projectile—maybe by accident, maybe by design. At any rate, some prehistoric woman thought to penetrate the ground, to hit the branch, and to increase the food supply thereby. Then some fellow threw a rock at some small creature, and bingo, new ways to get food! With these seemingly unimportant events an amazing process of transformation began that appears to be endless.

According to anthropologist Clifford Geertz in his book, *The Interpretation of Cultures,* with each new advance in human technology there was a corresponding alteration in the brain itself, as we developed the motor skills, the cognitive neurolinguistic tags, and the words needed to describe the new methods, tools, and materials. This caused culture to be altered, and this in turn gave rise to further innovations and brain growth. A mobius strip of endless development was initiated that has resulted, over the eons since, in the world you see around you now.

How amazing! How magical. Can you imagine how awed our ancestors must have been when someone was born among them with the capability of constantly creating innovations? Such people were most probably seen as inspired by invisible forces beyond the ken of the normal human. Such people as these were the first magicians, shamans, or sorcerers for lack of any better terms. They were creators, and did with their own talents in culture what nature did in the process of creating itself over and over in the infinitely varied forms of the mothering earthly environment.

There is a story among certain Australian aborigines about a time when women owned all the magic. They alone were able to create the ultimate masterpiece—a new human being. But it is said in this story that the men, in their fear of the women's power, stole the magic from them in order to gain control over it, and learned to create on their own. They reproduced their thoughts in the mediums of stone, bone and metal. It was with this turn of events that men rose to dominance as makers of weapons, tools, and other things. So the story goes on to say that there would come a time when women would take the magic back and things would return to balance.

The power of creation, of envisioning a pattern within and sending it out through the body to take on another form in the environmental substances, was at the root of what was once thought of as magic. Now it is something that can be taken for granted. And we've now reached a point where a woman can do this as easily as a man. Women can make, not only more people, but other things as well.

To have gone from spear points to nuclear missiles is a substantial leap. We have used language to embody the secrets of the creative process and gradually transform our environment and ourselves. For centuries the ability and capacity to be creative was seen as special. Few people knew how to create, and those who did jealously guarded their knowledge and conveyed it only to specially chosen inheritors. Now such knowledge is common knowledge.

The inventors and innovators have recorded their methods in written form in the last few centuries, rather than in the oral tradition that was the sole means of recording our mental patterns for ages. Now just about anyone with a little skill can obtain plans to make either spear points or fission bombs!

The magic belongs to everyone. Now the mediums we work with include ourselves, our cultures, our technologies. Of course, such has always been the case, but now we work on a vast scale beyond the comprehension of most individuals. We have a planet to transform. Embedded in this world is us, and we are the ultimate mediums for the creative process. We have done a good job creating the material cultures we live in, so now we need to act upon our own awareness to reconnect the fragments of the great circle of life into a singular whole once more. By extension, then we will connect ourselves as a whole to our immortal elements and to the source of the power of creation itself.

So let us now extrapolate this process to the planetary scale to see how it might be done. We are the creations of nature, the earth, the sun, and the incomprehensible forces that in combination are often termed the "Creator." The living earth is full of magic as yet not discerned. For we humans are, in essence, the memories, dreams, and imaginations of the world and its creator, whatever that may be. True, all forms record and reproduce certain patterns of activity. Stones are a geologic form of memory. Organic substances hold in their genetic patterns an incredible recording of evolutionary development that is older than the organisms themselves. For centuries humanity stored its collective knowledge in the medium of cellulose fibers, paper made of plants—now it is stored as digital bits in silicon circuits.

We human beings are thus the only form of being on earth capable of projecting our mental patterns onto external substances and creating a new environment. It is through human beings that the earth continues to develop the necessary systems of interconnectivity which could lead to the formation of Chardin's "noosphere," the web of consciousness which he felt would one day cover the whole planet and perhaps even extend beyond this planet into the heavens.

The planet is waking up, and it is through us it has come to see itself. The earth has seen itself and other planets, through human eyes, for the first time, only in the twentieth century, through the agency of human activity. The earth is becoming gradually aware that it has an identity in formation, and we are, by analogy, the cells of its brain, the medium of its mind.

The planetary identity is in a state of continual transformation. Our own development is a reflection of this process. The development of the fetal brain from undifferentiated cellular networks into specialized information processing systems shaped by and adapted to specific environments is a beautiful analogous process. A child, after two or three years of being conditioned and regulated by its mother (and the father to a lesser degree at first, a greater degree later), finally comes to be aware that it can organize and regulate its own activities, whereupon the child embarks on a career of conscious individuality.

We shape, and are shaped by, the environment. We interact with the environment and others to form our identity and our communities. We learn how to interpret the information of our senses and create our world. Yet, due to the limited bandwidths of our perceptions we see only a partial representation of what actually is. There are energies and interactions, previously unknown, that we become progressively aware of as our tools and technology extend the senses.

In this regard we must never lose sight of the importance of silicon. With silicon humans have created glass, radio tubes, transistors, and computer chips. It is by projecting our visions into and through this substance that we have vastly extended our ability to see the invisible realms now being charted by physicists. And it is into such substances that we are now channeling our memories. It is possible that human memory might one day no longer depend on human minds for storage. The accumulated knowledge of ages can now be recorded and transmitted digitally over great distances in moments.

And silicon is but one of over a hundred elements humans use to record the patterns of our minds. The denser substances of our material culture—denser than our own brains anyway—hold the standing wave fronts of our memory as the objects we see around us. Now if that's not magic, what is? And there's more to come as the planet wakes up and continues to project its own potentials through us. The living earth is becoming progressively more aware of itself, and the universal mind is finding itself within us. And at the same time, by a mysterious magic, we are becoming more aware of it, and increasing our ability to project our identity into the universe and across the cosmos.

Looking for Your Replacement

I was talking with physicist Colgate Darden in Columbia, South Carolina back in the mid 1970s. We were discussing the nature of change in physical systems, and the ways in which slight changes in the environment and the observer could have incredible and dramatic effects on the subsequent course of development within such systems. I felt that the laws of general systems theory would be applicable, and that, as Ludwig von Bertellanfy had thought when he created this syncretic discipline, the conception of change was generalizable across the artificial and arbitrary boundaries the various branches of science had attempted to set in place. Whether we are dealing with a sub-atomic particle, a molecule, a cell, an organism, a culture, or an ecosystem, the sources and outcomes of changes were a set of commonly experienced phenomena which could be described conceptually as well as mathematically in such a way as to reconnect the disparate categories of knowledge into a greater whole. In essence this was the beginning of what I call hologenics.

"I agree with you," he said. "In fact, I can tell you a little story that will illustrate why I think you are onto something that a young man with poetic and scientific inclinations might be able to explain. Thousands of years ago, on a high plain somewhere in what is now called Iran, or Iraq, or perhaps elsewhere—it really isn't that important where—the remnants of Neanderthal man evidently lived coincidentally with the rising Cro-Magnon. The Neanderthals were simple hunters and gatherers, but they were very clever. They had discovered the stone spear point, the principle of the lever, and perhaps even the wheel. But in their wandering lives they seldom replicated their discoveries or developed them beyond what was needed to maintain their pre-agricultural lifestyle. Apparently they had not developed the capacity for the kind of spoken language needed to retain and hand down their knowledge.

"The Cro-Magnon people, on the other hand, were not quite so inventive, but were more settled, domesticated animals, established agricultural communities, and were able to communicate using a much more complex system of sounds than their fearsome cousins who, man on man, were much stronger and more powerful, yet lacked the mechanisms for the complex vocalizations possible among their cousins. Due to this the Cro-Magnon were able to copy and reproduce the discoveries of the Neanderthals, and to develop means of providing a surplus of foods for their communities. Their population increased, and their ways of life gradually spread, forcing the Neanderthals into marginal territories and gradual extinction." He looked at me, paused for a moment to let the drama of the struggle sink in, then said, "and so it will be for us. It is our job to look for our replacements."

"Well, what sort of signs should I look for?" I asked, unsure of what exactly he might be referring to. "There are so many people and ways of life now that it's hard for me to imagine what I should direct my attention towards."

"Let me give you an example," he said. "Take my wife and her mother for instance. They can sit in the car in rush-hour traffic and both talk at the same time without any apparent misunderstanding! They are engaging in what I call 'dual communication', simultaneous sending and receiving of messages on the same channel. I don't know how they do it, but I think it possible that everyone might one day be able to." He laughed, smiled quietly, and asked, "Do you see what I 'm getting at?"

"I think so," I said, "it has to do with traits and differences that are subtle, but might be more adaptive in a new environment."

"Exactly," he replied.

I left him then and wondered: Could it be that there were people among those around me who had talents that, if they spread, could be the basis for the development of the next version of human beings? The prospect was a bit scary. I felt as though I were looking towards the sun, but that it was in eclipse, with only a beautiful corona of suggestion surrounding it. I called him back a few days later and told him of my fear. I was seeing a possibility, but that it was not clear. "Well," he said, "that's all right. The important thing is this: You might not find what you think you're looking for, but you will find something if you keep searching. Keep at it, and one day you'll find a way to get past your fears and describe what you see, and perhaps you will come across your replacement."

A few weeks later, I was talking with one of my mentors, Dr. Sid Varney, about my work, and my plans for the future. I was rattling off ideas very rapidly, telling him about what I thought of as my original inspirations as an artist, writer and amateur scientist, and where I hoped to go in my career.

"You know," he said, "I don't know how guys like you do it."

"What?" I asked.

"Well, you're like some other kind of race of people. You think so fast, so originally, that I just don't see how you do it."

"What do you mean another kind of race?" I asked.

"I don't know," he said. "You're just different. You see so much all at once I wonder why it doesn't blind you. Sometimes, even though I know what you're saying makes sense to you, I feel like I can't understand it. You know, when you talk about things like a thinking planet, a new race of human beings, or how you want to write a book and change the way people see the world—it's just beyond me."

I went on my way after that conversation, and the one with Colgate, unable to ever look around myself again, or into a mirror, without wondering 'who are we, and who will be my replacement?'

The Planet Remembers

The earth remembers itself through us, and by us enters into its emerging self-awareness suspended within the delicate filigree of silicon fibers, micro-circuitry, satellites, and other media of information exchange and knowledge generation. It is the dynamic and interactive fields of energy and their embedded signals surrounding us that link earth to sky. The mind of the world coalesces and precipitates from the sky to form the phenomenal realms where we seek some greater meaning. It is in this energy that we find some immediate awareness we are part of, which knows that, even if things appear chaotic to our scale of perception, they often have an enormous, yet highly organized interval, like music, harmonious and personal.

The noetic sphere of our awakening minds gradually clarifies and comes into focus. It allows us to look beyond the limits it forever encounters, limits that invite overcoming. We look out of eyes that have clearly seen the global outline of a growing consciousness of our unity and possible purposes. No matter where we pry and poke around, we continue to discover a seamless universe continually regenerating itself in every detail, timelessly and without end. To be aware is a great gift. To be awake is such a terrific accomplishment and a treat. If we can but use our awareness to guide our course and navigate through the shining dust and constellations we drift among, then our being aware in the earth has served a great purpose, and is, in any case, no less the wonder and joy to possess as human beings.

The inner voice of the world moves among and within us. This gift sings out into the sky unendingly, telling the stars of our great good fate. It tells of our potential regeneration as beings that sustain themselves and continue to be born and develop in the memory of the world and the universal mind.

We must remember who we are, that we are a singular being who exists in a living cosmos; that we exist within a living earth rather than on top of a dead rock; and that what we truly are is beyond definition and yet totally and immediately available to be experienced. Then, the earth itself can remember who it is, what it is, and that it too is alive and aware through all of nature, and especially through us, the human beings. It is the implicate order evident in every aspect of our experience; everything we know indicates that the universe is awash in waves and tides of infinite and immaterial intelligence.

The meanings we convey to one another ride the carrier waves of sound in the form of words. They go from mouth to ear and back again, from page to eye and back again. So too, does the meaning of the universe. It rides within us in the helical forms of DNA. The meaning of all life is recorded in our cellular memory, from its source in the all-pervading light of creation, through the various elements and beings which compose it as a whole and focus and reflect it back again to the source of its being. The universal intelligence is forever seeking itself, and in us has found its reflection.

We each appear to live and die, but that is just an appearance. What we are is pure, unfathomable energy. We are a luminescent being independent of material form. Our living energy is information that forever seeks out and renews itself as intelligence, awareness, wakefulness, and the shining which infuses all that exists. All we need to do is realize this, and we are immediately liberated into our transcendent forms, pure, immortal, and without limit. We contain within us the memory of the earth, the heavens, and of creation itself. Though we each seem to live and die, our genes are immortal.

Genetic Reincarnation

The genes are the enduring portions of human memory. They move from body to body, dancing in perpetual motion. They are housed in a fine cellular shell, which is further housed in specialized organs which make up the parts of a human body. And the housing doesn't stop there. We build our own houses, cities, and electromagnetic shells to protect and sustain us against the onslaught of disorder from the weather, sunlight, and other radiant sources of energy. We build to protect ourselves from those influences which break a body back down to its constituent elements when it has outworn its usefulness.

The genes are every bit as immortal as self-awareness and the consciousness of our being in the earth. The reflective and projective aspects of our sense of identity and kind of form make us unique creatures in a few ways of vast importance. One is that we record information in material forms. Our technology and information systems are evidence of this marvelous fact. The genetic form is repeated endlessly in the photosensitive chemical emulsion where our bodies develop, of which, in fact, our bodies are made.

Consciousness appears to be a general attribute of organic matter organized with a sufficient degree of complexity to bring about a necessary density of feedback circuits and systems. It has been a part of the earth's makeup since it came to be, and can express itself through a multitude of forms, all of which are very unlikely to appear in much profusion on a planetary scale.

That the earth remembers and is continually reborn is clearly evident in the consistency of the information in the combined genetic inheritance of our kind. That the variations of the human community remember themselves and are regularly, cyclically reborn is evident in the linguistic and cultural inheritance of the diversity of civilizations that occupy our world. That the soul remembers is obvious in the stories we all experience and tell to others of our personal, family, and communal past, our mythic origins, and our transcendental nature.

When the sperm and the egg meet, they mesh and replicate not only materially, but also electromagnetically as their energy fields also combine to infuse and organize the cellular potentials and define the developmental processes of the emergent organism. They pass on both the potential for perfection and transcendence, as well as the mutations and irregularities that the organism will be forced to deal with and resolve over time in order to survive. We are made of light that, as the poet Goethe noted, is "bent," "broken," "twisted" through the intelligently organized prismatic substances of which we are made, slowed down enough to contain and sustain self-aware life forms such as we are.

This inheritance of information—biological, cultural, and personal—is our stored fund of savings against disorder and chaos. It has the potential to order whole civilizations when articulated in the most appropriate mediums. We are continually reborn as a species. The potential personality types are likewise replicated repeatedly in many times and places across the ages of the world. We become immortals when we see beyond our egos, into our own DNA, and outward into the stars.

The genetic reincarnation of the human type is a biological certainty, and the rebirth of cultures in human communities will go on as long as language exists to facilitate the process. The collective spirit, soul, or consciousness of humanity is continuing always, even as you read this, to live, to spread, and to always prosper here on earth, and perhaps, one day, even beyond.

Cerebral Fusion

The scientists stare intently into their electronic eyes, watching for the breathless collision of atomic nuclei about to occur in the powerful circle of the tokamak ring. Out of the plasma soup will scramble a number of informational bits in the form of subatomic particles that sparkle in their infinitesimal realm in spirals and loops that tell the watchers what happened when the cosmos came to life fifteen or so billion years ago.

But how are scientists to accomplish such a magnificent feat? It took millions of years for human beings to develop the necessary abilities that allowed them to transform the substance of the earth and the light it contains into the material civilizations that have spread across the world for the last ten thousand years. People had to learn to harness the wild forces of water, wind, plant and animal life, and to live in large communities that did them as much harm as good.

They had to learn to harness fire, to use wood, coal, oil and nuclear fuels to feed their spread into all the environments and locales of the earth, and to refine the material elements and reorganize them into the forms of our manifest civilization. At the same time we humans have had to learn to minimize the destructive potentials inherent in this developmental process.

As food supplies grew, so did human populations, which then began to spread as they sought new sources of sustenance. One group ran into another and the cores of their cultures clashed and fused explosively, destroying the originals and giving rise to new civilizations. Cultural diffusion proceeded, and continues even today, especially as the telecommunications systems grow.

An artist sits in the twilight seeing, through insight and the voice within, the images of two bodies of information. They are brought together in a scintillating collision that lights up the mind with unique possibilities. A new fusion occurs. Original ideas emerge to light, and possibilities previously unseen become clear.

As a child begins to fuse the sounds most heard and often repeated in its surroundings within the mind, the language comes to life within, which makes the child able later to read and take part in the memory of the culture. At the same time the language acts as a screen or filter, closing out a significant part of the sensory input as unnecessary for growth and development, causing the propagation of only those elements of experience deemed relevant to the familial and social body.

The English language, and its Indo-European mothers, is a categorical reductive language. It classifies and divides the world according to the rules of its own unique vocabulary, syntax, and grammar. It attempts to reduce the parts to convenient simplified relationships so as to make them easier to manipulate, and to increase our understanding. Unfortunately this reasonable rationality also excludes many important elements and relationships.

For this reason it is of great value to understand and incorporate into our thinking other approaches to knowledge, and especially those inherent in the traditions of indigenous peoples who still live in close association with the natural world. They view it as alive, and see themselves not as rulers, dominators and exploiters, but as integral parts of a living world and universe.

What then occurs involves the fusion of the cores of bodies of information of diverse cultures, religions and sciences. The patterns of meaning given off in the coming together are interpreted in the light of equations used to explore the subatomic realms of the physicist. Concurrently, they're interpreted in esthetics and the various forms of art, in accord with the systemic rules of harmony and balance between the elements of any composition that create and govern its degree of attractiveness to a beholder. We can see in what ways they might be recombined to generate new harmonic forms and relationships. This is the process of cerebral fusion, and is a mirror of the process of creation unfolding forever in every direction around us.

Through this process we are able to rejoin and reunify the apparently exclusive elements of the human universe and create a vibrant, continually renewed world with ever growing strength, integrity, complexity, and order. As we fuse disparate bodies of information, we are able to discern in the cerebral sparks that fly the primal energies and parts of which we are made, which join us in the common experience of being human.

Critical Mass in the Information Pile

When explosive, especially radioactive, elements combine, the elemental resonance of the parts generates so much excitement that the mass fission results in a great release of radiation and noise. If this process gets beyond the containment vessel, it is one of the most destructive forces in nature: the atomic weapon. Held under control, although dangerous and demanding, it is a source of great power and energy.

Scientists have recently, using the process of depolymeization, accomplished the next evolution in energy generation. But the storage problem must be solved. Humanity must deal with both the benefits and problems of a universal source of power. As we move through the twenty-first century, the unprecedented growth in population and attendant pollution will have to be confronted. Fusion has also been developed to the initial point where it is possible to envision its use as an energy source at some future date. Hydrogen fuel development might provide a partial relief, but will we survive long enough to utilize this potent fuel? Can we capture the sun itself and convert its radiation into enough energy, at a low enough cost, to make it a feasible alternative to nuclear sources?

The combined elements used to bring about nuclear containment on earth—the "pile" of elements—are dangerous at best when placed close to each other in such a way as to create a critical mass. They join in the fission process and the controlled explosion is used to generate power.

But when atomic nuclei are fused and brought together under controlled conditions, the process creates a nearly inexhaustible supply of energy without the problems associated with the storage or disposal of toxic wastes. Or we can strip the oxygen from water and produce hydrogen as a fuel. These will be the next developments in the human capacity to capture, store, and use the diffuse solar energy stored in the elements by releasing it under controlled conditions for the benefit of as many people as possible.

We likewise combine sounds into novel patterns represented in symbols. We use recording devices to add to the storage capacity of human memory. This results in the gradual development of a critical mass of energy in formation. The piles of knowledge join and give off static—expressed as the heat of confusion, and the turbulence of change as more disorder makes the social system less predictable—and the system reforms and goes through a transformation, a change of state, a redefinition of boundary layers, which define a new, expanded or contracted sense of identity, as they fuse. The information pile explodes, and the chaos must be brought under control once more to preserve the integrity of the elemental core.

As it is in the social sphere, so it is in the minds of the members of social bodies and in the planetary mind which contains and sustains them. From what appears likely, the improbable arises. Without a corresponding change in the process of articulating and interpreting the changing relationships between the systemic elements, a body will disintegrate and chaos will rule. Death comes to the incoherent body, be it the result of bombs, sickness, or confusion.

This is the reason for the emergence of hologenic thought and planetary mindedness. These expanded views provide a frame of reference to use in ordering and channeling the way the shape of the world keeps changing, both within and without us. The shapes of nations, languages, and technology continue to shift towards confusion. To remain clear about who we are and where the exploding critical mass of the information pile will take us, we need look no further than some of the many ways the planet thinks about itself.

The Thoughts of Cities

The city falls from us like rain falls from the clouds. Technology precipitates from our mind's interactions with the places we gather and live and grow. The great thinkers, those who have changed whole civilizations, have emerged from the thoughts of cities. And we, those who live in them, are every bit as much a part of the thoughts of cities as they are a part of our dreams of life.

Spiritual giants have moved among us. Buddha, Christ, Lao Tzu, Mohammed, Zoraster, and Confucius, bringing vast populations to their knees in prayer to the unknown. Renaissance thinkers in the West—the likes of Luther, Calvin, Newton, Kepler, Galileo, Copernicus, Gutenberg, and Da Vinci—helped us gain the ability to master information and materials in ways both dangerous and beneficial. The creators of industry, science, atomic power, and computer systems have brought about planetary revolutions as their ideas have spread.

From within us these came, just as have the cities and all they contain. The work of many generations and elements has come together in these shining monuments to civilizations. Urban centers have acted as both fertile grounds for the growth of knowledge and breeders of pestilence. Such places also give rise to energy producing reactors that generate waste products deadly to humans for thousands of years. They become places which kill many, even as they act as incubators of brilliance. No matter how hard or long we work on our cities, they are forever on the verge of collapse.

Even cities have life cycles, for they are but expressions of the living beings who build and inhabit them. But like all things man-made, they are not very efficient and generate great volumes of toxic waste and human misery. From the smallest village to the greatest metropolis, human communities gather into concentrations that create sore spots, inflammation that can invite and cultivate the grossest poverty and degradation, where the energy of human beings is brought to eventual ruin.

Some of my American Indian friends talk of how modern people's feet seldom touch the ground, how they are protected by so many layers of civilization from the earth and sky that they are not part of either. They say this is what makes a human being empty, a lost soul adrift in the confusing cross-currents of modern life in the cities. It is the Native American sense of identification with the ancient homeland where their ancestors' bones enrich the soil, where their beliefs and ways of life came into being, as told in the myths and stories of origins and timeless heroes and villains, that makes them strong still. Their cultures exist as a part of the earth and the elements, rather than apart from them. Indigenous peoples across the world know the power to be drawn from a rich cultural tradition that is part of an ancient landscape. And they also know that alienation and separation from the land destroys identity and degrades culture.

The thoughts of cities are disturbing and disorderly. They shine in us and draw our children like flies drawn to decay. They stimulate and inspire our visions of a new world where we can go to make anything imaginable happen. Perhaps soon enough we will have cities in the sky, take vacations at orbital hotels, or send vast cities across the interstellar distances much as our pioneer ancestors crossed the unknown lands, and like our descendants might cross the skies as science fiction writers have imagined.

But such thoughts come at a great cost. This kind of growth is accomplished at the expense of the environment and must exact a price from us in disorder, disturbance, and distress. Cities lead to environmental exploitation as the population grows and local resources and supplies of goods run dry. This requires the intensification of the development of political structures to deal with the inequities that come to exist as the social order stratifies and tensions between classes increase until rectification is demanded and equality guaranteed.

Tension results in institutional structures which become more rigid over time as they attempt to stave off disorder and chaos. They eventually become inflexible, leading to the breakdown of order, descent into turbulence, and disintegration or reformation in a different form. The city seethes with the forces of transformation, and the demand for adaptation. It can never be completed. As long we live, we live in groups, and as long as we continue to grow, we make environmental demands that cause the buildup of pressures that eventually must either be released or lead to explosions or fusion. The ultimate outcome of living in concentrations of fifteen to twenty million people depends upon how well contained the shock waves are which are generated by the turbulence within the individual, society, and its institutions.

But the city also represents the way in which humans adapt and grow and contribute to the development of sustained holographic forms of memory that make an integrated universal mind possible. Cities are a form of memory storage. They are the way the earth remembers much of what we humans do. They house our cultural and genetic information and allow us to remember who we are. Our identity depends in some way on the existence of cities. No one is free from the activities going on in our city-covered world.

They live day and night. They never close. They have those who attend them whether it is dark or light. In fact, they generate their own light. They are thinking of us in their libraries and telephone systems. They are dreaming of us in their televisions, movies and computers. They are helping create what we will be next.

Spiritual Politics

How then are we to enter into the healing center that allows us to regain our balance, when it is destroyed by our own growth? How do we continue to grow without hurting ourselves? What must we do to help ourselves define what we are going to be? While speaking with world-renowned peace scholar, Johann Galtung, telling him of the ideas presented in this book, he looked into my eyes in silence for a time and then responded thus: "So what you are suggesting is a time to come when what happens as people communicate with one another is that god is looking at god through our eyes, yes?"

"Yes!" I blurted. I was excited and amazed that he had gotten what I was attempting to express in one sitting.

"The problem is that your idea will remain no more than a think-piece at this stage, for you have described no policy, or political process of implementation whereby it could be put to use," he told me.

It was then and there I realized he was right. It was obvious that the infectious nature of prejudice, racism, aggression, religious differences, and nationalism is not to be overcome easily. Maybe it will never be resolved.

Another friend of mine, a Zen monk who meditates most of the time but enjoys gambling as a contemplative activity as well, and I were talking one day and came to conclude that the world would either 1) have a golden age wherein all people come to work together to solve common problems, 2) experience a continuing sort of "10% solution" in the world, where no matter what happens there will always only be that statistically predictable group of "enlightened" persons who are needed to guide others in the way of life most beneficial to their community, or 3) have to meet our "evolutionary expiration date" and, having fulfilled our evolutionary function, mutate into another sort of organism, or cease to exist as a distinct species altogether. We agreed that no one knows for sure what we are becoming or what to do about it, and that humans unfortunately don't usually do anything until something goes wrong.

Some positive signs that we are likely to achieve more widespread global-mindedness rather than go extinct include the following. National boundaries continue to shift and merge as ideologies change throughout the world. Some of the international arsenals are being dismantled and smelted into tractors and other tools that will sustain life rather than destroy it. The emergence of the Internet makes national and other boundaries more permeable.

The world economy will eventually stabilize in response to population controls put in place by the women of the world in the 21st century. Chemical birth control and medical abortion have resulted as men have attempted to control population and impose their reproductive will on the women. Great imbalances in gender ratios and ideologies have resulted. On the one hand it is perhaps of value to have slowed population growth somewhat in some parts of the world. But, on the other hand, population control inhibits our collective developmental processes and movement towards the ultimate and inevitable crises we will have to face as our numbers reach the limits of our resources and capacity for energy production. Women must eventually be more intimately involved in resource development and use, and base the number of offspring their community can sustain on environmentally sensitive criteria.

It is people, and the human spirit, that matter most. All beliefs and ideologies must be judged by the degree to which they are beneficial to the people who hold them as true. Lessening of resistance between the elements, and an opening up of relationships among various human communities must minimize division and fragmentation resulting from distorted communications. We need diversity to strengthen our adaptive potentials. But we need a certain degree of consistency from culture to culture to insure that all contribute to the process of creation from the individual, to the community, to the global sphere and the networks of information which bind it together in a dynamic unified interaction.

The healing center is within all of us. It is in the power of life that sustains us and stares out of us in mute wonder, which drives us to create ideas and project our consciousness into objects unpredictable and improbable. It is in the core of the individual being, within the sense of identity of the community and its commonly held language and culture, and in the unity of the global environment. Through all of these parts the integrated mind comes into focus and the elements are clarified and unified. Our wounds are healed and our identity becomes well defined.

This planetary revolution, this internationalization of civilization, starts with each person developing, in his or her own way, a global perspective that can be applied within a local context. There is enough knowledge, and it has spread through the global information system far enough to provide assistance to any who seek the broader view. We must live and work within ourselves, our families, our communities and the environment that gives us our bodies and lives, in such a way as to bring together in lasting union our previously disparate and separate social and cultural elements.

This is the solution and the end to the planetary identity crisis. It is the beginning of a shining global intelligence, of a spiritual politics, of an equitable and stable economy, that extends through all of us, from the core of our beings to the edge of the universe. It is what we are, and forever shall be, in the planetary mind as we expand beyond our world and extend our awareness towards the distant constellations.

Once we have achieved the kind of mind expansion required in the process of fully coming to understand who we truly are, then, and only then, can we begin to accept and realize that beyond our individual and communal lives there is an even greater life of which we are part, yet which is forever beyond us. We can experience it, but we can never completely know or express it.

We must redefine our relationships to one another, the planet, and the universe. We must literally reach beyond ourselves, beyond the sense of otherness and the feeling of separateness, alienation, and loneliness that can infect us if we indulge our individualism too much, if we are ever to realize and act on our potentials.

The remainder of this book considers some of these matters, and attempts to sketch a broad outline of how we got to where we are, and what this indicates about where we might yet go. There must be a means of implementation, a process whereby knowledge can be applied and utilized. Politics and spirituality must ultimately become the same thing as we continue our growth towards an integrated sustainable global civilization of great beauty and diversity.

IV

On America

WE LIVE IN AN INCREASINGLY FAST-PACED TIME. The validity of the concepts upon which our nation is based are increasingly denied by the lifestyle which we are living. We think of ourselves as such a great country, with good health, long life, prosperity, family values, love for others, sharing, unity of purpose if not thought and belief, and a shared world view that makes us strong and powerful in world affairs.

But wait! Hold the train! We rank well down in the world listings for infant mortality and life span. The Swedes keep more of their infants alive in a socialist state. The Japanese outlive everyone else in a homogeneous culture that frightens and intimidates us. A few percent of our population controls most of the wealth while the working classes endure wage slavery by the hour and watch as their earnings continue to plummet, eaten away by inflation, an increasing tax burden and a forever escalating cost of living.

Our aging population is being forced to wait longer than ever to retire. Retirement age goes up to sixty-seven in 2005 and to sixty-nine by 2010. The social security net is threatened by the federal government's irresponsible misuse of the funds.

Our divorce rate has leveled off at about 50%. It was up to a nearly two-thirds failure rate for first-timers, with an eighty-five percent failure rate for marriages where both parties had been married before. We say the vows, we preach the lifelong commitment, while all the while practicing serial monogamy. We are not a bio-chemically monogamous species. Marriage is a social, economic and cultural institution based upon outmoded customs fouled with a romanticism that detracts from the actual contractual nature of the relationship.

More than two-thirds of our children will experience a single-parent household in their lives. Women are robbed of their power to control the domestic sphere by the demands of the economy and the marketplace, as well as the patriarchal social codes—so much for the nuclear family. When women lose control of reproduction and the family, the social fabric will be torn beyond repair. The demands of the modern world have forced familial implosion and the results are vast and devastating—in terms of both human and social expense and a growing irresponsibility on the part of absentee fathers, welfare custodians, and apathy on the part of all.

Increased mobility, declining fertility, dual income households, biased, anti-male and anti-family divorce laws, and a host of other factors combine and conspire to make ours a nation of uncertain, alienated, emotionally fragmented and mentally disabled youth who no longer have anywhere left to look for direction or models. They watch the television and see sex and violence. They view the movies and see the wicked prosper. They look around for some sort of coherent and moral model upon which to base their behavior and find only fragmentation, archaic religions which are preached but not practiced, and alienation in the home and workplace as people work only for money rather than pride and purpose.

The fragmentation of American identity and the gradual passing of the dominant culture of white Anglo-Europeans is a continuous sort of degeneration. We are all passing into the realm of being minorities. This, coupled with the rise of the military-industrial corporate state that is actually a global entity, which has no honor or respect for nations or peoples, whose sole motive is greed, and its sole goal profit, leads to a "damn the people and the natural world" attitude. This situation has led us to the brink of ecological disaster. It is not so clear or evident, and it will not be apocalyptic.

The water will slow to a dirty trickle as global weather changes. The land will be blown away in a new series of dust bowls. Continued reliance on petroleum will cause more pollution and expense, increasing the tinderbox situation such that more conflicts will break out, more people will be displaced and become violent.

The Hindus say this is the Age of Shiva, the Kali Yuga, the time of destruction. The Iroquois say we are on the path of death. It is the period when the evil in the world must consume itself and take down any and all who cannot bear the rigors of rapid adaptation to continually new conditions, ongoing degradation of nature, and the purposeful exploitation of human and animal populations for the sake of the bottom line.

The Christians await the return of Jesus, the Jews the coming of their Messiah and his Zion, the Moslems the spread of the jihad to all nations. Allah el Allah! There is no God but God? Whose God? Which God? What universal church? Catholic? Zion? Moslem? Hindu? The demise of the infidels and institution of Islamic law? Whose kingdom of heaven are we talking about here? Just what are we to make of this?

In times like these the demagogue and the utterer of baseless, old-hat generalizations stand ready to take over where the politicians, preachers, and popes leave off. So, where is the unity of thought? Where is the sharing when nationalism and religion are at the root of so much of the conflict in our world? How much longer before the militant fractional minority is able to engage in nuclear or bio terrorism?

Why does America continue to insist on sticking its nose in other people's civil wars? What are we doing in Bosnia, Korea, Japan, the Mid-east and elsewhere? George Santayana's comment regarding how "those who don't learn from history are doomed to repeat it" has fallen on increasingly deaf ears. Several thousand years of recorded civilizations in evidence have fallen due to their inflexibility in the face of conditions they have created: their economically crushing militarism, imperialism, colonialism, expansionism, and their unchecked fragmentation. These do not impress modern peoples who have lost any sense of history, know little about their past, and really don't care as the spirit of the age drives them to make more money regardless of consequences.

Just what are we now, America? How can we as a people incorporate planetary mindedness into our society and relationship with nature, and universal concepts into our personal lives and culture in ways that will help sustain, empower, and contribute to our longevity? First we must face who and what we are in fact, rather than in myth and fiction. The shared mass hallucination of culture propagated in our homes, the stories we grow up with, the media, and our religions must be taken apart and put back together again in a different way. Maybe then we will be able to figure out where we fit into the world to come, who we are, and be able to act now to enter into it.

Thomas Jefferson suggested that the government should be peacefully replaced every twenty years or so in order to keep the revolution alive. But he also noted that the people will always tend "to endure a tolerable tyranny rather than embrace an unknown freedom." The status quo has become our king, our bellies a god.

The illusion of stability and comfort are rotting away the core of our integrity. Our system is on a headlong course towards chaos and then, either renewal at a higher level of order and complexity, or dissolution in the miasma of conflicting impulses. We are on the edge of the world without a center the poet Yeats spoke of, the world out of balance the Hopi have decried, the world we all know inside is about to befall us regardless of what we are told, or what appears to be the case.

So read on, follow me deeper on a search for the singular unifying and most powerful conception available to counter this trend towards destruction. We must draw upon the knowledge of our elders and ancestors, who gave us life as we continue theirs. We must look into the past with open eyes in order to reform our vision of the present so as to more effectively insure some sort of habitable future for our descendants. Come on this journey. "Let us go then you and I," as the poet Eliot said.

Our Criminal Nation

So here we are, our criminal nation. We Anglo-European-Celtic derived barbarian hordes who like so much to travel, go Viking, robbing, plundering, overrunning, removing, and murdering whatever local resistance we encounter—yes it's us. "We the People," thumbing our noses at authority, doing away with kings and popes, freeing ourselves to be the thieves we are. Our Constitution is strong because it is made up of the freedom and land of native peoples we stole it from, and upon whom we committed genocide in the name of God and king. We simply invented an idea—Race—and used it to justify the exploitation, robbery, murder and mayhem imposed upon those viewed as primitive, savage, barbarian, heathen, uncivilized and therefore inferior. What one author termed "the white man's burden" was meant to name the sense of duty felt by those impelled to civilize those less "evolved."

Fine thing for a bunch of greedy crooks, debtor's prison inmate overflow, prostitutes, confidence men and women and unlanded gentry to feel, as those are but a few of the criminal groups from which a majority of early American colonists were drawn.

Frederick Jackson Turner noted the "frontier hypothesis" as a shaping influence in American history. Henry Nash Smith wrote of the notion of the "Virgin Land" and the way it molded hundreds of years of nationhood. *Manifest Destiny and the Metaphysics of Indian Hating* written by Richard Drinnon, and Vine Deloria's countervailing shout that *God Is Red* and *Custer Died for Your Sins* thundered through our national consciousness in the 1970s. The Puritan "wilderness" was more a reflection of their own confusion than a conception that mirrored the environment they transplanted themselves to when no one else in Europe would tolerate them.

We have but one holiday that commemorates the saving graces of our indigenous heritage: Thanksgiving! A day of mourning indeed for most Indian tribes left today. Were it not for the wilderness peoples having saved our Anglo ancestors we might be living in an Indian America today. But the Anglo-Europeans had what Mao Tse Tung later commented on as "power [that] comes from the barrel of a gun"—the metal technology useful for increasingly efficient human and environmental exploitation. So, the colonization of the allegedly "New" world, the juggernaut of empire entered into and took over what became America.

We feed the world from our genetically altered mono-cropped farms, fertilize the globe with the seeds of our culture and songs, and wire the planet with our electronic impulses, even going so far as to send our satellites careening across interstellar space into nowhere. We have sent out the signals of our civilization across the empty sky, made a sphere a hundred light years across full of the twisted nomenclature of our weird and beastly vision. And oh, have we ever profited, gotten rich while the sagging masses cried, lived in splendor while the poverty stricken billions have died for a crust of bread or grain of rice. We have so much to be proud of, don't we?

We are the World Police, weapons makers to every fearful little political entity whose time is but a puff of smoke, profiteers. Our power over empires is so vast we can break nations with a bold stroke of the pen in our Congress. We use our markets to buy and sell the world. Infiltrated by an obese greed, by fat heads full of hot air and gross words, inflated with our pride we form the conflicts, we shape the wars, we control the peace for our bank account's sake. Why do we dally in the civil wars of others? Why do we play the protection racket with the Japanese and Germans and Jews we've conquered? We do it to keep the stakes high, the steaks warm, and the red blood of American youth flowing wildly and freely towards a deadly but profitable future.

Population has outstripped global food production capacity, pollution is forging full steam ahead, the oil will soon run dry. The very elements of the nature we destroy will revolt against us, even our own cells. We will bring down the plagues, and no liberty, no talk of strength and freedom, no uranium or bombs will save us then.

We are a nation of criminals. We need to accept this, for it is our history and destiny. If anyone disagrees, it will do him or her no good. We are the body of evil, of greed, of destruction, of the beast of our own undoing. Let us enjoy our comforts while they last. Let us enjoy our health while it is still with us. We are getting old here in America. We are not replacing our lily-white selves. We are moving towards an economy of inheritance where most don't have to work, they only have to manage mom and dad's leftover insurance money, and where the stratified poverty stricken masses of youthful minority immigrants and laborers will put up with the social and economic disparity for just so long.

We will have to legalize death, make it an attractive option for the sufferers, give it away for free eventually, put euthanasia chambers in the malls and let the excess kill themselves for the rest of us. What a beautiful world, eh? We are its makers, you and I, all of our ancestors and relations.

How do we do anything about it? How do we reform our perceptions, language, culture, society and ourselves to "create a more perfect union"? Let us first consider some of the foundational ideas upon which our criminal nation is based, deal with them in a straightforward fashion, and then look at how we might rearrange our conceptions, values, beliefs, attitudes, and behavior into a more benign configuration for the sake of coming generations.

When we accept, understand and embrace our criminality we can begin to heal the schism at the heart of our civilization. We can only change what we know, love, and accept about ourselves. We can only be as big as we dream, as great as we imagine. We, the people, must extend our identity so that we are once again the human beings, the first people, the dawn people, and the ones who have always been.

By adopting planetary mindedness we just might be able to create a new legacy that is socially conservative, which preserves natural resources and the environment, and which offers a means of renewal and diverts us from the destructive path we tread now. We can give up our criminal system and its ways when we've faced, and gotten over, our fear of what is beautiful and right in our soul. In real freedom we can then live and prosper, rather than an illusion of freedom sustained by force of arms, paid for with blood, and dedicated to the proposition that all men are equally gullible suckers ready to be fleeced!

The Fallacy of the Idea of Race
and Failure of Civil Rights Law

Just what is race? It is commonly defined as a "biological classification based upon physical characteristics." But it is far more than this merely scientific statement suggests. Race is a conception of otherness, a classification based upon perceived differences. It is not a thing. It is an idea about social relationships. There has never been any substantial proof offered, any clear dividing line provided—socially, physically, chemically, or even microbiologically—in support of the validity of this idea. Skin color plus money equals race.

Anglo-Europeans, have, for five hundred years, used this idea to dehumanize those who are not derived from pale-skinned, temperate-zone stock, who are not descended of the original inhabitants of what is known today as Europe. White people simply invented this idea—Race—and used it to justify the robbery, murder, genocide and mayhem imposed upon those viewed as dark, primitive, savage, barbarian, heathen, uncivilized and therefore inferior—primarily because of the color of their skin—and how this influenced the development of other perceived differences.

Just who are the Anglo-Europeans anyway? Where do they get off telling a whole planet of others that they are inferior if not of Caucasian lineage? Eternal immigrants, wandering, lost souls who don't know where they're from, their sources or origins, they appropriate whatever land, beliefs, or origins they find convenient and available wherever they happen to settle for a while before continuing their marauding sorties into territories not yet penetrated.

Look where this has led. In modern America this idea has been so twisted for political uses that we have a social policy and laws today based upon a false notion, fabricated by invading hordes of heartless, landless barbarians, that was created as a conceptual tool to support and justify criminal, immoral, unethical, and simply evil conduct.

So, where in the world did these people get the idea that they are superior, and that they are Christian in their origins? They are not Semitic or Arabic peoples with roots in the Middle East. They did not come from Jerusalem. They are not even but distantly related by lineage and genetics to the Jewish, Moslem, and early Christian populations. Studies of the ancient forms of their languages suggest that they are primarily from northern India, originated in the Hindu lands of the speakers of Indo-European languages.

But they left their homelands long ago, and there's the suggestion in their behavior that they know this, and deny it. Yet they longed so much to return to their ancient sources that the colonial enterprises of five hundred years ago suggest their actions were an attempt to renew their ties with their original ancestors, as much as it was a search for gold and spices and converts to the adopted religion of Christianity.

Little wonder then that it was so easy to use Middle Eastern originated concepts of religion as tools for exploitation and colonialism. The turmoil of the Dark and Middle Ages in Europe was, in part, overcome by the Crusades and the attempts of the Catholic Church to appropriate the distant homelands of people from whom the tenants of their adopted religion were derived. The bringing together of the feudal lords of warring European municipalities eventually led to the development of modern European states and nations. But Vatican City and the Pope still stand on the mountain, dark lords from the ancient world, influencing the destinies of five hundred million members of their fold of ignorant sheep. Of course, the eight hundred million Moslems who surround them, and the several million Jews with whom they claim spiritual affinity are not necessarily well pleased that they even exist.

Beyond this you have the three billion Communists who consider these antique belief systems to all be invalid attempts by corrupt states to control the working masses of the world and exploit them for profit.

What's amusing is that Communism was derived from an English anthropologist's (Robert Wallace) Euro-centric misinterpretation of Iroquois Indian culture and politics. A young Karl Marx then reinterpreted the political confederacy of new world aboriginal peoples. The great German political philosopher had left home, and gone to continue his studies and writings at the London library. He found Wallace's monographs and settled down to create his greatest works after being fired from the German university where he had worked and been deemed unable to meet their expectations for an academic professor.

What's even more amusing is that the very ancient knowledge preserved in the oral traditions of indigenous peoples for forty thousand years, and from which all modern expressions of spiritual sentiment are derived, is still evident among so-called "primitive" peoples even today.

Indigenous people's primary view of human relatedness and experience is notable in its consistency and variety—and especially in its lack of any construct we can relate to the idea of "Race." Most of the world's peoples developed their worldview over long periods of isolation within localized environments where they differentiated out into the multiplicity of cultural forms still in evidence today. Incorporated into their culture specific views was some idea that marked each people as unique and different from others. Most often such ideas were useful in the maintenance of cultural integrity and group and personal identity. They were not used as an excuse to kill off whole genetic groups or economically exploit others for the most part. It took the development of scientific racism to bring about the emergence of a pathogenic worldview whose goal was the complete extermination of others who happened to be in the way of Anglo-European expansion and colonialism.

Race as a concept is a remarkable and notable fallacy. It has led to racism, racialism, genocide and the modern variants of civil rights laws and affirmative action in America. Civil rights laws are based upon this fallacy, and they have, essentially, failed to alter racist and ethnocentric views. They do, in fact, help level the economic playing field, but they do not address the basic flaw in American thinking about groups currently (though perhaps not for long, or for always) in the minority. Race does not exist except in a theoretical sense. It is a product of the categorical imperative and reductive thinking used in biological classification. Such classification says nothing about the fact of our common humanity, relatedness, biosocial history and need for truly equal rights and equality under law.

What does differ among people are their cultural and ethnic identity groups, languages, and ways of life with their attendant perceptions, values, beliefs, attitudes, and behaviors. But these cannot be effectively used as a basis for the creation of true equality. All people must be acknowledged to be equal as human beings before laws can make them so—and if they are so acknowledged, no fallacious laws are needed.

Each people developed their worldview by drawing upon universal and instinctual understandings about how to relate to and influence the natural world so as to insure and maintain favorable conditions and plentiful resources. First peoples based their identity and sense of security on the locally developed views of the human place in the environment. Their rituals, ceremonies, traditions and such came to be as they provided a means for the people to relate to the ecological sphere in a positive and productive way.

But, in the process, each group entered into long-term isolation from others and became exclusive, monolingual, and resistant to others whose views might disturb the natural balance. They began to think of themselves as different from and unrelated to their neighbors.

Do I ramble? Do I digress? Do you have any idea of how closely related we all are? No individual human being is genetically more than a fiftieth cousin to any other. Can you begin to see that our diversity—of such great genetic and cultural value in that it allows us to more variably adapt to environmental and social changes—has been used to help us destroy a part of ourselves? We can have a vast number of varied groups, customs, languages, cultures and the like, while still acknowledging that we live in the world together and have a common vested interest in maintaining ourselves and nature for future generations.

The use of Race, as an idea, as a basis for social policy and law, as a motivator for human relations, is a massive failure, and about as sensible as seeking commonality through appealing to religious sentiment or national boundaries. We share a world. There is only one human race, composed of endlessly diverse elements and peoples. Racial differences are a fallacy, but a powerful one, used for five hundred years to justify much evil, exploitation, and conflict. We must alter our language and remove this construct, and the perceptions that attend it.

The lion and the gazelle drink from the same river, but they have never been at war.

Spectacles and Slavery

Many peoples throughout history have practiced slavery. Not until the establishment of the American colonies was it used for wholesale economic exploitation of millions of people for the sake of profit for a limited few. Most pre-modern slavery was a form of servitude. In many societies one could work one's way out of this condition, by marriage, service, or other socially acceptable means. Some slaves could engage in combat or games to earn their freedom.

Most peoples taken as slaves, excluding those taken for use as sacrificial lambs in the old blood religions, were forcefully assimilated, or incorporated into the body of the people who took them captive. Otherwise their presence would serve as a disruptive, divisive or destructive influence and so they were killed. But slaves were rarely used to turn a profit. For the most part slavery was more of a social, and less of an economic, institution. There were other ways to deal with issues of class and social status besides exploitation and murder of others.

Even today there are millions of people enslaved in various parts of the world, especially Africa. The buying and selling of humans is an ongoing problem. The undeveloped world is where most of it occurs.

The Cherokee people had yearly games, as do many other peoples. Athletic contests were a means, other than combat, to establish one's prowess and social position, and to work one's way out of slavery. Whether in ancient Greece or Rome, or in the Celtic or Asian empires, physical abilities have always been respected, especially when such abilities were applied on the battlefield or in the sports arena.

Is it not curious that this is still the case today? Slavery is still widespread in many forms. We are, in fact, wage slaves for the most part in modern America, toiling daily for an unknown, unseen "owner." So we need spectacles to provide an outlet for pent up aggression, to inspire the kind of identification and affinity for the home team that creates a sense of community and gives us something to talk about when we finish with the weather. "Hey, how about them Bulls?"

And is it not of interest as well, how our current American sports scene is still the community within which the issue of racism rears its ugly head in subtle ways? Are not the people who are in control of athletic teams still bearers of the antebellum title of "Owners"? Although the "slaves" today can make millions of dollars a year, the owners are making even more money, still economically exploiting the physical prowess of their minions as in the days of old.

Things have changed, certainly; but the dungeons are still underground in locker room locales, and the players must wear the costumes, follow the rules, and be at the beck and call of the owners, who just happen to be, for the most part, Anglo-Europeans intent on using them for their profit, just as was the case in the early days of American plantation slavery. The terms and roles are still clear. And we all know who still owns whom.

Marriage and the Mammal:
The Scent of Fertility and Mating in the 21st Century

Love is easy. Commitment to tolerance, helping another become what they choose, and sharing space and time are where the compromising work and effort lie. Compatibility is only the beginning. Agreeing to resolve issues, communicate, be at peace in the process of defining the nature of being together—these are the difficult issues to be dealt with. In nature no such concerns exist. We respond to the scent of fertility in the air, do the mating dance, give or receive the seed, and reproduction goes on without social or cultural intervention. But in our lives as social beings we must deal with the culturally mediated means of achieving reproduction and creating the family and social unit.

Marriage as an institution is only useful for legitimizing children, establishing rights of inheritance, and other customs that are primarily the products of patriarchal society. Male and female can relate well enough without the artificial strictures of economic, legal, social, and moral bonding associated with primogeniture. Such are unnecessary for relationships to exist, for people to get together and reproduce, and are generally useless other than in their value as social and economic formalities. The true nature of the act of marriage is primarily to be seen in the area of contract law. Any two people, of any gender or background, can draw up a contract defining their obligations, duties, responsibilities, and benefits to one another as relates to their common interests under the law.

We are all supposed to be equal under said law, but each of us tends to get the legal counsel we can afford. In nature the strongest will win. In democratic society we can each get whatever measure of justice we can afford. Such is the nature of modern American society. And this is the same whether in the personal, social or economic spheres of our legally defined nation.

Companionship and sex and closeness within the socio-cultural institution of marriage are justifiable if and when it works, but it rarely does. The ancient and outmoded rules of the patriarchal nuclear family dictate a forcible obligation. This is hardly the "ideal" or most desirable state of relationship. Our moral codes are hopelessly archaic and lead to no end of conflict and confusion in American society. We have no uniform or homogeneous moral code. We say one thing and do another. We lack the tightly woven social fabric and conditioning methods of cultures with histories and tradition dating back thousands of years.

We no longer practice marriage as it was intended. We practice serial monogamy. Sixty-five percent of first-time marriages will not last. Eighty-five percent of second marriages where both have been married before will also fail. We stand in front of our families, friends, church and civil officials and recite meaningless promises we may intend to keep, but usually don't. We deny the purely contractual nature of familial relations under the patriarchal model and then end up with a society full of fatherless kids. We are turning into a nation of bastards. And marriage continues to exert itself as a form of legal slavery.

This is the result of our refusal to face our moral emptiness, and the failure of such social institutions as marriage, family, social welfare, women's rights, the war on poverty, race relations and civil rights, and other attempts at institutional regulation of instinctual behavior. Archaic codes will not fulfill our vast need. We need to reconstruct human perceptions and rules to fit the actions we commit, and which most benefit us, and dispense with the rest. We need a behavioral morality based upon practice, rather than a conceptual morality based upon archaic belief systems derived from middle-eastern origins, and other places and times—which we don't live by, and which are not good models of, or reflections of, our actual actions. This is a daunting task, but is no hindrance to the planetary mind in operation within each of us. Beyond the I, we are. This we must see to go on. Adapt or die. That is natural law. Treat others as one's own self is the basis of social law.

Our perception of gender relationships must be overhauled and clarified to shake out the dust, to revitalize the clarity, and to strengthen the process of male and female bonding in such a way that it truly contributes to social stability and cultural integrity. As it stands, the institution of marriage is fraught with problems and violates natural law. It is not adapting to our needs in the twenty-first century.

In a matriarchal society there are no bastards, no illegitimate children, little in the way of child abuse, and men are not, and have no interest in being, on top all the time. All children are members of their mothers' families and lineage groups; the male role models are the mother's brothers and father; and the father hasn't the burden of owning or controlling the material, social, and political spheres.

Instead men work within their clans for the betterment of the community. They play their part in organizational and administrative tasks, but are appointed to, and remain in charge of said work at the discretion of the female elders and clan mothers. Perhaps there is a lesson in this. But are we ready for it? Can we take it to heart? Can you catch the scent of fertility in the air and engage in natural relations outside of social law? Not likely—but let's next look at how this came to be and what has resulted under the rule of men.

Marriage and the Mammal II:
The Scent of Fertility and Sex as Commodity

We live in a patriarchal nation of irresponsible bastards and power-less women. Just look at the papers. Child abuse, household violence, dead-beat parents who pay no support for their offspring, illegitimate children, single-parent homes, welfare motherhood, male domination in the social and economic spheres, and severe socioeconomic stratification which puts many children at risk, and leaves society in turmoil. One must follow the law or suffer the consequences. How did this come about?

Many thousands of years ago women provided three-fourths of the food in hunter-gatherer societies. They literally ruled the roost. Three-fourths of the world's cultures were matriarchal, matrilineal, or generally organized along female dominant lines in both genetic and political senses. Woman had the power, they owned the magic, and they made sure the children were taken care of, as they knew for sure who their children were—while the men never could be sure. They controlled mating by chemical and other means based in our instincts and matriarchy.

Much has been written by such wonderful writers, for instance, as Jared Diamond, about the various advantages and disadvantages inherent in various mating strategies. One thing is clear. We humans are not biochemically monogamous. All formalized familial bonds are socially and culturally derived as a means of controlling instinctual human nature, and are imposed, not natural as such. We practice serial monogamy, and no bold promises or public declarations or government issued documents will change that, especially not in America, where the social stability, familial and community responsibility, and economic system are structured so as to deprive women and children of the power they once had under natural law.

When plants and animals were domesticated and the man began to follow the plow and play the corral rather than chase the wild beasts, women were, over time, relegated to a position of being viewed as household property; and primogeniture as a social construct formalized the disempowerment of women, and put the men who owned the food, animals, and weapons in charge. Women became prostitutes and slaves to the male domination and were viewed as property in the male household.

The process anthropologist Calvin Martin called "Intensification" led to a gradual build-up of excess material wealth and political power as non-inheriting sons were put into the military forces to control the population. It concentrated in larger and larger groups focused on trade rather than living harmoniously with the forces of the natural world. Daughters became part of a man's household property, to be bought and sold as he deemed fit. Sex became a commodity. Culture overcame nature. Man overcame woman. Law overcame instinct. Marriage became another type of slavery, a sport wherein males exercise dominance to the disadvantage of females, society, and the environment. The Iroquois call this way of doing things the "way of death." This is something we will return to in a later section.

The Welfare State and the Fall of Women

What ever happened to women? In prehistoric times women primarily ran seventy percent of the world's societies. The women were the creators and preservers of the community structure and integrity of the family. So what happened to cause them to lose their power?

Before about ten thousand years ago, all cultures were living the indigenous lifestyle based on hunting, gathering, some wild cultivation, and pre-technological agriculture. After that time in the mid-east there arose the early forms of agricultural civilization based upon domestication of plants, animals, and development of primitive metal technologies. This led to the development of civilizations that were in direct and dramatic contrast to the diverse cultures, language groups, religions, and social forms based upon living within, rather than upon, nature. Today we have around three hundred nations in the world, rather than the thousands of localized cultures that existed in prehistoric times.

Patriarchal civilizations, or cultural systems, which emerged in many places—such as those which developed among the Semitic peoples, which later spread to the tribal Indo-Europeans to the north, and later Celtic civilizations, who further developed the system—led to eventual overpopulation, intensification of environmental exploitation, development of political economy, codified legal systems, materialistic belief systems, and surplus labor forces. Among males, this resulted in forced service in military forces engaged in territorial expansion. Among women the result was far worse: virtual slavery, as they became part of patriarchal household property and ceased to provide the majority of food and primary processing of raw materials into finished goods. Trading economies displaced their function.

When men run the world, it ends up being disadvantageous to all but those with the money and power. The primary goal and direction of production and commerce becomes profit and control facilitated by the creation of weapons of mass destruction. These weapons are the only products modern America makes and sells at a profit. They are used to dominate the rest of the world and make it a place where corporations, courts, and nation states are the central forums for the development of political, legal, and social policies aimed at limiting the access to goods and services for all but the few men of means.

So, this is what happened when women lost their power. Marriage became a form of servitude, lineage was related to the male lines, and thus, bastards abounded. In turn, the development of the welfare state was necessary to take care of fatherless children and powerless mothers who have no clans, no control over the uses of the environment, and no recourse for redress of grievances save that of the patriarchal state machinery.

We live in a nation today where up to eighty-five percent of the children born will at some time experience, or be in contact with those who must endure the tragedy of, a single-parent household. Millions are consigned to food stamps, the welfare rolls, and the impoverishment that results from poorly constructed child support systems based on patriarchy and law rather than matriarchy and human needs.

We cannot control the reproductive urge without taking a chance on unpredictable results. Amniocentesis has led to excessive abortion of female fetuses. The one-child policy in China has resulted in the wholesale slaughter of female offspring and an imbalance in the ratio of male to female adults that will have repercussions for the next generation or two—a marriageable adult ratio of sixty percent male and forty percent female will lead to incredible social problems.

Birth control is handled by altering female cycles, with the use of condoms, through the process of abortion, and by various other means. But any attempt to limit our numbers simply delays the inevitable. We need to face our world problems head on and reorganize ourselves globally in such a way as to allow humanity to reach its maximum number in order to learn what our optimum population might be. Women must control their own fertility, not men.

As the oil runs out, the food supply dwindles and the economic systems crumble, problems associated with imbalances in population dynamics will increase, and we will be forced to be reactive down the road, rather than being proactive now. The uneven distribution of goods and services worldwide in accord with the profit motive will ultimately lead to increasing conflicts. The uneven ratios of male to female will further upset the scene. Our instincts have gone awry.

In prehistoric times the male knew by sight, smell, taste, touch, and other sensory means when a female was receptive and fertile. He could directly sense the rise in body temperature, the shift to alkaline chemistry, the brightening of the eyes, reddening of the cheeks and lips and other signs of fertility. But that has been lost due to the advent of multiple means of concealing fertility, and the cultural mediation of reproduction in the form of socially approved methods of mating and marriage. It's in the best interests of women in a male-dominated world to either hide their fertility or appear to be fertile all the time. Sexual power is the only power left to the women, as they have been robbed of their power over the material sphere and dominance in the social realms of home and community.

In such a world, sex has become a commodity, something to be bought and sold, owned or tossed away, embraced or rejected on a whim. Our moral conceptions are no longer in line with our behavior. We do not follow nature or the law. The result is confusion and conflict, and an uncertain nation of fatherless bastards, powerless women, and impoverished children.

This will continue as long as modern societies insist on maintaining the socioeconomic institution of patriarchal marriage as the main form of cultural mediation of the natural reproductive impulses. But a time will come when the conflicts which are the result of this will no longer be avoidable. Today in America the institution is breaking down. The war between the sexes takes on a whole new, frighteningly bizarre meaning when we consider the widening role of women in war.

Military Arms in Our Mercenary Country

Should women go to war? Should all citizens, both genders, bear arms in defense of their country, at home and on the battlefield? This is a controversial argument being dealt with in the American military today.

For the most part we have become a mercenary country, a profitable producer of military hardware—so much so that we continue to involve ourselves in the conflicts of other nations at great expense. We attempt to prevent lesser powers from producing the same weapons of mass destruction we profit so handsomely from! We promote our position as the protector of democracy when we, in fact, are no more or less suited to control conflicts abroad, to produce and sell weapons, than any other nation.

We sell protection. We are a criminal nation, and have always been a mercenary country, bent on protecting our interests at all costs, and by every means available. We protect our friends and attack our enemies— either militarily or economically. We attempt to control the marketplace and regulate commerce globally to shore up our sagging economy at home. We grant or take away access to our markets to control the political and economic systems of nations whose interests differ from our own. And now we are considering whether or not it is best to send women into the fray.

Our military has different sets of rules governing women at war. For instance, women are allowed to return to the rear and shower once every three days, while men must endure two weeks of sweat and stench at a time. Physical training standards also differ. But when it comes time to move the heavy equipment or lug the ammo and guns, it is primarily the men who will do this, while women will be allowed to carry less and be coddled more at the expense of the males.

While it is true that women make better pilots, have better hand-eye coordination, color discrimination, and a more generalized approach to the taking out of assigned targets, they rarely have the aggressive tendencies produced by testosterone and adrenaline in the male soldiers. Men have always been killers—of game and enemies who threaten the territory they view as theirs—and enjoy it. Women are more interested in preservation and maintenance of the whole group. They seem less prone to glory in the wholesale slaughter of the enemy.

It seems then, that even if policy statements could somehow equalize the differences between the genders, we would still need to deal with the matter of what happens when women are taken prisoners. This seems to be the central issue. Women are subjected to the same evasion and escape training as men, but they will on occasion be captured and brutalized in front of the men in order to gain control over them. They can be raped and forced to bear the offspring of the enemy. This is a powerful inducement. Men can be manipulated through its use.

I see the possibility of women in front-line infantry combat units as dangerous at best, devastating at worst. Women may be able to use power and weapons as well as men, but they cannot be as useful as male combat ground soldiers unless they are sterilized. Thus our mercenary country further disempowers the women, making them into choiceless victims of our male warrior mentality.

Why instead don't we change our view to be more in line with the female tendency to avoid conflict if possible for the sake of the whole, to distribute goods and services more equitably so that all the children have equal opportunity to survive and succeed?

It's true. We can't just give up war and weapons. We need to be able to protect ourselves and kill our enemies should they attack us. But we have become so hesitant to use our ability to destroy others that we are not the respected military power we were even a generation ago. America must either be willing to wipe out the perceived enemy if they resist, or cease to be involved in the conflicts that arise in the world. Until we elect leaders who are able to see and act upon this need, the respect of other nations towards us will continue to decline, and all the weapons in the world won't replace it.

Illegal Taxation and Citizen-Government Competition Leads to Social Insecurity

During the sixties in the U.S. the government returned to the Jeffersonian idea that it is important to not tax the working people as this puts government into competition with the citizens for investment capital. The Founding Fathers incorporated this idea into the Constitution by insuring that the central government makes money by duties and tariffs and the general regulation of interstate and international trade alone.

The personal income tax was instituted in the early twentieth century to aid in funding war efforts. The politicians boondoggled the public into believing that it would not be a long-lived situation. But it seems to be a rule of politics that, if the public gives more, the government will find ways to spend more. Thus, programs were initiated, such as veteran's benefits, social security, and later welfare programs along with Medicare, Medicaid, and a host of other entitlements. It's interesting that the Supreme Court never refuted the matter of the legality of taxing personal income. The government has no more right to tax the citizens than the citizens have to own weapons when they are not members of the militias of sovereign states liable to be called to defend the nation at any time. Citizens are/have been allowed to keep firearms so that they may obtain food, protect their families, and check the natural tendency of governments to dominate the people.

Now the entitlement programs are being eroded away. Two generations have been taxed out of any possibility of starting their own business, have been forced into wage slavery in a world actually run more by corporations than by national governments, more for profit than ideals. For all this the people have paid into a social security system that will be eaten up by poor fiscal practices before those who made their contributions are ever able to retire.

Numerous plans have been put forth to alleviate this likelihood, but they will be as likely to fail as to succeed. We are entering an economy of inheritance. The baby boomers will leave their children upwards of $30 trillion! By 2050 more than a third of the population will be retired, and a third will be underage children. Inefficient distribution of goods, services and resources, and other inequities in the economic system, unconstitutional appropriation of monies from the working citizens, and questionable social policies do more to encourage than alleviate inequality. A new approach must be developed that is based on sound principles of systems management rather than the greed of politicians and corporate CEOs.

Drugs and American Culture

Why has the war on drugs been such a resounding failure? Why have we pumped billions of dollars into interdiction, prosecution, and imprisonment of those who traffic in and use prohibited natural substances? We do this while simultaneously allowing the unregulated use of nicotine, alcohol, and caffeine, and while refusing to face the fact that many of the most hard-core drug addicts are those who take prescription drugs. How can we say, as a society, that mind-altering plant substances have no place or use, when most human cultures have been making use of them for at least forty thousand years?

We are culturally in a state of denial. Until we get at the causes of the use of mind alterants and understand their natural purpose, we cannot arrive at any kind of answer to these questions. Peter Furth, in his wonderful little book, *Hallucinogens and Culture,* chronicles the prehistoric and historic traditional uses of plant substances to induce mind alteration. Perhaps he doesn't really delve enough into the social value of such substances, but he does justify the study and value of understanding and accepting that it is natural for us to engage in the use of substances that dissolve our preconceptions and allow us to view the world from another point of view.

We live in a society with little in the way of dramatic rituals of passage into adulthood. In such rites one's limited identification with self and individual ego is stripped away to the point that the primal powers and nature of being human come forth in organized patterns of understanding that allow the individual to transcend localized knowledge. This knowledge gives a people their sense of identity, belonging, coherency, and cultural affiliation.

We need not look far to find people who have the means of marking the passage into expanded, more mature understanding. Our own indigenous populations utilized numerous plant substances to induce altered states for the benefit of individual growth and the maintenance of cultural integrity. Even within the current frame of reference, we have situations such as that in Amsterdam, where the use of marijuana is socially regulated in the same way as prostitution, for the public good. It is neither legal nor illegal. It is simply recognized and accepted as a natural activity, like sex.

Other substances such as morning glory and other seeds, various mushrooms, cacti, and many plants throughout the Americas have been used over time—many still are—for both spiritual and social reasons. Why is this so? In part it is a matter of recreation—not just playing for fun, but of actually recreating the primary state of mind, free of limiting definitions and boundaries, which is natural to human beings early in life. We thus recreate the sense of innocence, purity, wonder, unity, and identification with the infinite that is at the root of any healthy psychology.

When times become confusing, when society is in upheaval, when conditions change rapidly and dramatically, we can experience a sense of disorientation, alienation, uncertainty and a breakdown of identity resulting in all manner of psycho-spiritual ailments and disharmony. These conditions can lead to distress, disease, and even death of the individual human being.

At times such as these there needs to be a means of getting outside the temporal flux and flow of events, of going beyond the geographically defined boundaries of self and culture. We seek and need ways of inducing altered states of mind where new responses, revised information, or just useful changes in perspective can be experienced in a safe, non-threatening manner. There is no way to stop people from finding ways to alter their consciousness. Whether the means are socially sanctioned or not, prohibited or regulated, outlawed or accepted, denied or subsidized, the end result will be the same. People need to be able to change their point of view sometimes in order to facilitate effective adaptation to new or changing conditions in the social and/or natural environments.

In America more man-hours are lost to respiratory ailments due to tobacco smoking each year than to nearly any other single cause. Many thousands of people die due to alcohol consumption, or the use of prescription drugs. Yet we allow and support the use of these substances while denying the rights of twenty-five million users of marijuana to be able to indulge themselves without becoming criminals. We likewise refuse to develop ritual, ceremonial or other uses for hallucinogens and place them in the same class with addictive narcotics like heroin and other opiates. We blame the users for the results of our social denial of responsibility because society lacks organized, controlled settings where such substances can be used without fear of mental breakdown, overdose, arrest or imprisonment.

We are wasting time and money on trying to stop the unstoppable, while we ignore the need for better understanding and regulation of what will be used regardless of the law, social sanctions, or disapproval. We create biased commercial messages bordering on propaganda in support of prohibition and attempt to call it education. At the same time we give only a partial picture of the causes, nature of, and proper approaches to the uses of mind-altering substances. We ignore completely our denial and refusal to face our socially sanctioned uses of addictive, cancer-causing, deadly substances promoted by the powerful lobbies in our governmental system which have a vested interest in their continued use. Here, I refer to the alcohol, tobacco and firearms lobbies, and to the American Medical Association, and other such professional organizations, whose members continue to profit greatly from the development and imposition of treatments for the negative results of substance abuse—both of legally sanctioned and illegal mind alterants. Add to this the profits of the drug companies due to prescription drugs, and it is easy to see why corporations and governments have a deeply vested interest in controlling the public's state of mind and perceptions.

The good doctors and mental health professionals will cry foul at this accusation, but it won't change a thing. No doubt individuals are not nearly so culpable as the system at large, as the corporations, as society as a whole. Just the same, there is no way to change the impulse in human beings that drives them to seek diversion or escape from the intolerable conditions of an insane world. It's the only way to find alternatives sometimes. Unless we perfect our society, workplaces, homes, and educational systems the stresses that result from wage slavery, poverty, personal psychological imbalances due to poor diet, bad relationships, and lack of equal opportunity, our people will continue to live and die in ways not necessarily in their ultimate best interests.

Either we find a way to use mind-altering substances in a sane manner, or we will continue to be used by the pharmaceutical, alcohol and tobacco companies. We must utilize every tool nature provides to seek answers and alternatives to our current dilemmas, or the coming generations will continue to do themselves and one another harm. Mind alterants are not, in and of themselves, dangerous. What's dangerous is to deny the causes and value of their use and attempt to force our population away from using them through continued prohibition. We already did that once—it didn't work with alcohol, and it won't work with marijuana, psychedelic mushrooms, cacti or other benign psychotropic hallucinogens.

On Death in America

I must now write on the issue of elective self-termination. A few years ago the book, *The Final Exit,* described a number of means whereby one might kill oneself. It was a best-seller within a week of its publication and release. It . This indicates that there is a vast untapped potential market for products and services which are related to the desire of the human and social being to have a choice in the matter of when and how to die. There are, of course, inherent cultural biases which preclude the rapid institution of corporate euthanasia franchising—but come it will. Nobody seems alarmed at the incorporation of mortuary and funerary businesses on a national scale. It seems, for the most part, that most people just don't want to face death and talk about it.

Numerous moral arguments have been advanced against the right to die. Prominent among them are those which focus on the "wrongness" of the act, on the moral and ethical prohibitions issued by various religious and belief systems which consider "life" to be inherently "sacred" and death by election or with assistance to be unnatural. Others comment on the potential for abuse should society tacitly support such actions. But moral arguments are in the province of the personal, and have no place in the legal and ethical arguments that must become the sole focus of the debate. The Quinlan case decided the issue and declared that choice regarding death was a matter of the constitutional right to privacy in acts and decisions regarding life, liberty, and the pursuit of happiness.

Unless we are willing to declare that suicide is an act of premeditated murder, that warehousing our elderly is a form of institutionalized killing, and that sending soldiers to kill abroad is a type of moral atrocity, then we are going to have to face the fact that we need some sort of constructive social dialogue on this matter so as to put death in its place as a moral option and a legal choice.

Three states have recently struck down their bans on "physician assisted suicide" and the Kevorkian trials have found such bans unconstitutional in Michigan. Oregon voted in an initiative in 1995 to legalize the process, but the state Supreme Court issued an injunction against the will of the people. The law was agreed upon in the public domain, but experts suggested it was ill-advised and not clearly enough or fully enough defined to be practicable and legal. As of 2002 dozens of Oregonians have elected to end their own lives, and no signs of abuse have emerged there, or even in nations that sanction the practice, such as Holland.

Twenty states allow the terminally ill to die with physician assistance, although it is neither a legal nor an illegal action to take on the part of either patient or doctor. Let us consider some other relevant facts as regards the right of the individual to elective self-termination for the good of individual quality of life, the benefit of community and society at large, and as a part of nature's way.

In many American Indian cultures, and among many other indigenous peoples, it is considered appropriate for the elderly who no longer are able to contribute to the community and have become a burden to elect to remove themselves from society to return to their source. In Japan hiri-kiri is an ancient custom, and elective self-termination considered in many instances an honor and duty.

Abortion is legal throughout many parts of the world. Amniocentesis is used to determine gender and as a basis to elect for termination of the fetal expression of the mother's life. The termination of unwanted, defective, or undesirable neonates is a common practice among many of the world's peoples. Poison, suffocation, abandonment and other difficult means are used to implement fetal or infant death. Infanticide is even more common than abortion historically. A defective, disabled, or malformed newborn had to be done away with for the good of all as such persons would draw an unfair amount of resources from the community.

Further, how can we honestly consider these approaches as different from the socially sanctioned, federally subsidized, choice of smokers, alcoholics, prescription drug addicts, and others to slowly terminate their lives—is it not but a matter of time? Nicotine, alcohol, and opiates, to put it succinctly and simply, are deadly. We kill to live, destroy plant life in the act of consumption and use, kill helpless creatures to consume their flesh, stalk and hunt and kill fellow mammals without a thought for their right to live. Ethnocentrism is a real problem, but specicentrism is one of even greater proportions. Who are we to decide that any life form should be terminated? We elect as a society to allow the termination of the life of a species every minute! If we can choose to terminate others, then we can choose to terminate ourselves.

Once again, empty and fallacious moral constructions play their part in the creation of the perception that our tendency towards specicentrism is somehow justified and allowable. We believe that killing of others in war is right and moral and that supporting social programs and policies that lead to death is acceptable. Such constructions pose the greatest impediments and most daunting problem that will be faced by the providers of products and services for those who choose elective self-termination.

Such providers cannot be held liable for the actions of the consumers of their good and services, any more than the producers of guns, whiskey, and pills are held accountable for the use of their issue. Future businesses, which arise to address these issues and needs, will require good lawyers to construct contracts, plan estate matters, deal with new insurance issues, and define our responsibility towards the client/consumer.

Initially it will behoove them to focus on and direct their concerns towards the terminally ill. Effort should be directed towards the development of policies and procedures to govern the ways and means the election is conducted. It must be determined who will be eligible for licensing and responsible for termination, and the affairs of clients must be handled posthumously to accord with their own, their family's, and the society's wishes.

A time is fast approaching when legal decisions will override moral codes and the "phenobarbital drive-in" could become a possibility. But we can avoid such perverse facilities by deliberately engineering new institutions in such a way as to facilitate elective self-termination in a regulated, dignified, and legal manner. Doctors, lawyers, and other attendants must be fully incorporated into the process. In the end the choice belongs to the individual. This choice is absolute, in fact, regardless of law. But we must still consider the needs of society and the associated rights of the family and community. We must at the same time provide the optimum terminal experience for our citizens, and allow the rise of businesses which address the needs of those who elect to die by giving them a means of achieving a dignified ending.

With a revised worldview we can reconsider the experience defined as death and reconstruct our understanding of it without the burden of ancient metaphor clouding the issues. Death is liberation into immortality. True liberation is freedom from form. Our value as living beings is to enrich our earth, to absorb the radiant experience in the realms of light so as to give it back to the source of life when we cease breathing and return to our original state. We must learn to view death as the definitive release of our life force into the unlimited, undefined, and unmanifest energy that is the power of creation itself. We must allow anyone, who chooses to let loose their life, to do so by choice at whatsoever time they please. We have a right to choose when our work is done. If we are incorrect, that is not a problem, for built into the universe are processes whereby life will continue regardless of the choices we make. Call it rebirth, return, reincarnation, or whatever pale metaphor might be useful, but the power of life is forever seeking itself. It always returns to its original state of perfect unity with the greater whole, a unity that our sensory systems are far too limited to see or comprehend.

America must take the helm in this and become the nation where real choice, freedom, and liberty make the pursuit of happiness a reality in life as well as death. But first we must clear our minds of the spider webs and dust, free ourselves from the tyranny of history and look into our potentials. We must discern the path into what we will become, rather than limiting ourselves only to what we have been. In order to do this we need a corrected understanding of the planetary mind, a globalized intellect, and universal consciousness.

This process of becoming more understanding of life and death in the twenty-first century is the hope of America, and ultimately, of all peoples. We must be on the leading edge, or we will fall so far behind we will become the unenlightened laughingstock of others.

V

The Constellations of Thought

JUST HOW DO OUR THOUGHTS FORM? How does the brain work its magic of generating and storing information? Our brain cells are interconnected, directly or indirectly, with one another. By extension those cells are connected as well to aspects and elements of our external environment that our sensory systems are able to detect and respond to. A useful analogy is that of the night sky and the stars we see spread across its vastness. Our thoughts are similar in that the multitude of points are joined together in what one might call the accretion discs and constellations of thought.

The neural system has the ability to hold an electrical charge—capacitance—generated in the process of experience and retained as a memory or engram. The process of thought is dependent upon the activation of ions of crystalline, organic metallic compounds such as calcium, phosphorous, and potassium. Information processing depends as well on the interaction of over one hundred chemicals, hormones, peptides and other neurotransmitters and neurologically active substances. These substances leap the synapses chemically and propagate the movement of electrons between orbital levels in the molecules of thought.

Signals are sent along the neural pathways and stored as electrochemical potentials. These potentials are definitive within the brain, in that they form a sort of mental shadow that is at the root of consciousness and sense of self or identity. The electrochemical systemic organization as a whole is greater than the sum of its parts. It generates the multi-level reactive, receptive, reflective, and projective layers of awareness that lead to our sense of self and the development of a unique personality based upon genetic inheritance, cultural heritage, and personal experience.

The mind is not digital, but is the analog source of binary mathematics. The mind is not like a computer—computers are like selected parts of the mind from which their designs are derived and magically projected into the substances of our external reality! The difference being that in the human system a switch, or neuron, can be on, off, maybe, perhaps, almost, and a host of other configurations that amount to variations on signal attenuation. These variations give the mind its capacity to create vast constellations of thought within the tiny space of the human cranium. The human brain is said to have as many connections between neurons as there are stars in the sky. Something along the lines of ten to the twenty-third power!

Chemocoupling of neurotransmitters generates infrared energy, or heat. The energy is used in the process of electromagnetic capacitance and the generation of vibrations in various bandwidths and frequencies. These vibrations are stored as holographic patterns of potential awareness that are multi-modal, syncretic, synthesized formations. They are charged energetically and they can repel, attract, or remain neutral depending upon mental state. We can gather a charge in the form of memory, hold it in a static or active form, let it loose or connect it to others in a variety of expressive ways such as action, speech, or thoughts of either negative or positive type. When we discharge our energy, it can feel like either a loss or a relief, depending on the polarity of the initial accretion point and the positive and negative sum of the stored impulses which gather around it as a static charge which we call energy in formation, or memory and thought. As the charge and spin of the molecules of thought change, so does the configuration of the energy held in formation. As such, if we alter the process, we transform the product into a new form.

Interstellar dust gathers around the gravity well of a star in formation, or a black hole, to create the galactic disc, or solar systems. In the same way our thoughts are formed into various shapes and configurations that form the many structural and super-structural formations of everyday thought. They may also combine at higher levels of integrity, most evident when under the influence of naturally derived mind-altering substances, or in meditative and visionary states induced by any of the variety of conditions or practices known throughout the world in the various spiritual traditions. Included as well are the enhanced states of awareness achieved in dreams and visions.

Prayer, chanting, exercising, deprivation of sensory or biological systems, meditation, or shamanic endeavor are all but a few means of inducing enhanced or altered states. The spheres of neurologically active electrochemical, ionized/molecular, and elemental compounds that accrete around the poles of stored energy in formation are the basic components of the thought processes and self-awareness.

Sensory, perceptual, cognitive, and social functions are integrated in the six outer layers of the neocortex. These layers interact to create the spheres, elliptical mirrors, or lenses, and other shapes of thought. The points of accretion are vector resultants, or foci, which, in sum, generate the "shapes" within, and of, the neural net that is viewed as the composite whole. The greater whole is made up of the component elements, or energy in the multiple thought formations of the personality. When a high capacitance charge, or set of charges, is stored, it can be polarized negatively or positively, or be neutral, and act as the general foci around which incoming signals accrete or gather.

There are quite probably aspects of the thought processes operative even in the deepest quantum domains of subatomic particle exchange. We still have so much to learn about the nature and makeup of self-awareness. It will be a while before we can come to any solid conclusions regarding the actual nature of consciousness. But we know enough now to change our minds as we please, if allowed to.

Different mental states and frequencies of neural activity in the bandwidths from 1.5-28hz activate different elements and compounds of energy in formation in the processing system. Each systemic set of frequencies almost has life of its own and can often be experienced as different facets of the fragmented self. We are all full of our ancestors, our families, friends, and experiences, a multitude, all jostling and hustling about to express themselves. They all seek to rise into our awareness and gain our conscious awareness of their being.

Those processes of thought with a high frequency and amplitude are most usually negatively charged and give rise to the least pleasurable mental states in the beta range/bandwidth of 14-28hz. In the alpha range, from 7-14hz, the components of the processing are generally neutral, balanced and free-form. The low frequency/higher amplitude signals of the theta range between 3.5 and 7hz are usually positively charged and give rise to reverie, dreams, visions, and intuitive insights. Signals below the delta wave threshold of about 4hz are associated primarily with sleep and unconscious processes related to psychological integration, bio-chemical harmony, social unity, personal healing and cellular regenera-tion. Such unconscious functions are necessary in the maintenance of systemic organismic health and vigor. There are also quantum dynamic fluctuations that occur during the interactions between the individual body and the material and cosmic elements of physical and radiant substances and energies.

If the resultant of compounded signals—generated internally by the processing system, or in response to external phenomena—gives rise to a vector set of neural firing that is not clear in terms of signal strength, integrity, and vibratory qualities—then the ability to think, reflect, and project thoughts in the form of action will be limited, compromised, or rendered dysfunctional. One cannot in such a case "gather one's thoughts together." Cosmic dust gathers around black holes to form galaxies that act as gravitational lenses. Likewise, within the mind, specific points of significant polarity tend to gather cortical elements which are like dust and can cloud or distort the thought process. If the lens is twisted, bent or polluted, the result will be clouded thinking. How are we to overcome this problem?

This is the point at which the science of holographic thought begins—with the development of awareness that allows one to influence and control the constellations of thought. Awareness permits us to control the accretion discs, spheres, and other shaped systems within the universal and human minds, and their dynamic structural integrity. It is an approach to mentation that is systemic, integrative, holistic, and generates health in the mind-body. In short, a holographic model of thought is "hologenic" in that it allows us to create a healthy means of seeing the greater whole.

The use of prescribed chemical compounds—psychotropic drugs—to affect consciousness, as utilized by the allopathic medical and psychi-atric community, on occasion does more harm than good. Drugs are used as a means of control, to manipulate those who resist being forced into the mainstream. But psychotropic drugs are rarely used to expand awareness. Mental health professionals under-utilize the hologenic approach. The failure to use mind-expanding drugs, especially those derived from plants, results from a fundamental primitivism and misunderstanding regarding how the brain and body interact electromagnetically to create, preserve or destroy the basic integrity of self-consciousness, personality, behavior, and society as a whole.

The tenets, and useful natural substances, of shamanism are viewed by said professionals as superstitious holdovers from prehistory and ignored. It is for this reason that some mind-altering compounds—harmine, mescaline, psilocybin, and lysergic acid diethylamide to name but a few—are said to be of no value and made illegal, and why the war against drugs has failed so miserably. Sixteen billion dollars a year has done nothing but put users of plants in jails, while thieves and child molesters walk the streets.

There are simply very few theorists or researchers who are enabled through training, inclination and institutional or economic support to create effective and adequate models of consciousness. A quantified self-awareness would allow a broader, more general, and far-reaching modulation of our understanding of the psyche so as to create healthier, happier people. As such, there has only been a limited exploration of the higher neocortical processes and states of awareness, and activation of unpredicted, yet probable, potentials for super-systemic expansion of consciousness into the planetary mind and a more universal awareness. This will change, as new conditions require human beings to adapt by searching for alternatives to their current paradigms. We need new worldviews, and a deeper understanding of holographic memory and planetary consciousness.

A revised view of what it means to live and die—both of which are more descriptive metaphors than facts—will be required in the twenty-first century. We must review our personal, cultural, social and national identities and reconstruct our values, beliefs, and attitudes to accord with the true nature of our experiences.

We must base our morality upon our actual behavior rather than upon either the antiquated concepts inherited from the ancient world of our ancestors, or the incomplete and fragmented worldview created by the modern materialist and scientific societies. We in America are the nation least burdened with history and tradition. We are therefore most suited to develop a revised approach to life in a world where the separate individual, the nation-state, and the industrial corporation are all fading into decentralized, perhaps even irrelevant systems. That this is so is evident in the development of the Internet and cyberspace, as we gradually discern the outlines and features of the relatively unexplored electronic continent.

We can, in fact, influence our collective understanding of the nature and relationships of the energies and elements of the universe within our brains. Different cultures named the constellations differently. They came up with a variety of names for, and explanations and definitions of, what the stars are made of, how they are organized, and the ways in which they are related. We must likewise create an alternate, improved way of looking at ourselves, the stars, and constellations within and without, which recognizes, describes and defines clearly our inter-connectedness, however we name it.

Love, the Word, and Gravity

The word is alive! Everything is alive, animated, in motion, flux, regardless of what our limited senses might say to the contrary. As long as the word is part of the operating system of a living being, it is a part of the fabric of life and is the source of our sense of self-awareness. The word is the means by which knowledge and culture are preserved and information handed down from one generation to the next. It is the beginning of our capacity for consciousness, the mirror into which we look to reflect on ourselves and our condition, and the power which joins us together in groups through the sharing of languages, ideas, and worldviews.

Have you ever taken a moment to wonder what this means? What is it that causes certain sounds to join together with others to create words? What is "meaning"? It is mysterious indeed. Earlier I explained that meaning is "energy in formation, for energy that is in formation is meaning-full, while energy that is not in formation is meaning-less." Our sensory systems are made to sense deviations from a flat line, or norm. When vibrations occur, our senses receive the impressions and our perceptual systems allow us to determine whether or not there are any patterns, or formations inherent in the signals we receive. Our cognitive capacity then cross references the patterns with others in our memories and gives them a cognitive tag, definition, or word by which we recognize the event and set of relationships indicated by the signal. Of course, by that time the initial event is long over, but we'll get back to that later.

There is a power, force, or energy in the universe our physics defines as "gravity." It is the power that joins things together, which holds them in a unified state in relation to one another, and by which our universe develops into the diversity of the cosmos.

When people, or other creatures, care for each other, and join together in couples or groups, we tag the powerful feeling or emotion critical to the bonding process, "love." This power is evident in the human realm that joins us together in personal relationships, families, communities, cultures, societies, and nations. It is the power that binds us together.

Do you see where this is going? The suggestion here is that the living words of language have inherent in their being the power of gravity! This energy is the source of the common bonds of attachment that bring people, ideas, and star systems together. Love, the Word, and Gravity are all manifestations of the same power! This power has all the characteristics of attraction of the physical force that binds things to one another universally. Gravity is the Love of God—speaking metaphorically of course. And the Living Word is the expression of God among man. That is the metaphorical significance of the archetypal or mythic figure of Jesus—as well as Buddha, Lao Tzu, Mohammed, and other world teachers of various times and places. Such beings as these are expressions of the intelligence of the whole universe back to its very beginnings, insofar as it can be represented in the human being. And each of them invoked that power in their followers in order that they would develop likewise into fully conscious beings, and achieve even greater awareness as this knowledge spread among all peoples.

This knowledge is therefore not the property of any single group, religion, or people. It is the primary knowledge that predates all subsequent forms of awareness, religions and worldviews. It has been handed down for millennium, from the source of human experience and conscious awareness. It is the means whereby we, the human beings, are joined together with and in the universe in the great sphere of living, breathing, and being in existence.

Somewhere along the line, as we traveled around the globe and settled into differing environments, we developed unique ways of seeing, relating to, and remembering ourselves, others, and the world and universe around us. These actions were consistent with the language, customs, values, beliefs, attitudes and traditions of the people and environment within which we developed. This led to a growing sense of difference, of separation, of disunity and conflict—a misperception, unavoidable, but remedial.

We think we are each separate individuals, cultures, nations, religions, etc. But in fact we are still joined in the great circle of life, and all of our conceptions have come from the spheres of energy and matter brought together by gravity in the physical realms, love in the human realms, and the word in our individual and collective minds. It is a singular force, with a variety of manifestations. We are joined, we human beings, whole, perfect, one, complete, by its power.

There are also powers at large in the world that seek to encourage our divided selves and perpetuate our sense of differences as a basis for action towards one another. These seek to bring us to the edge of conflict and disintegration for the sake of profit and power. The conflict between the forces of love and hatred, and the political and economic powers of need and greed continues. The capacity of those who support division to imbue our world with fear of scarcity, of going without, of being alone grows daily. Each of us must find the way within our communities, our nations, and ourselves to overcome the illusion that there is not enough for everyone. We must know that we need not be at odds in order to live, that armed and economic conflicts are not the only means of protecting ourselves.

We must return to an understanding of our inherent unity, of the fantastic gravity, of the power which joins us together as human beings. We must understand and accept the word of love, and the capacity for integrated intelligence that is universal, and brings all things together to work in unity in creation. In this way alone can we regain our primal innocence. We can understand and overcome the sense that the divisions we are aware of (which are the results of the limitations of our sensory systems) are in fact nonexistent!

A planetary reformation of consciousness is called for. This is both a return and advancement, to take us into the eternal life of creation and the intelligence of the universal mind. We must look beyond the fear of death, deprivation, and suffering that results from a belief that we are wanting, that we are lacking, that we are not all here together to perform our parts in the singular dance of life on earth and in the cosmos. There are forms of awareness and knowledge that predate all the modern worldviews and religions. They preceded our science and technology. These ancient ways and words are still with us, albeit in the dilapidated and archaic, broken-down versions that divide us today. These partial and divided forms of understanding are the "way of death" noted earlier. To overcome them we must return to the way of life and encourage a reunion of all human beings. In this way we can get past the materialism and folly at the core of modern civilization.

How might we do this? We must construct a morality and understanding based upon unity and upon our human inheritance over the ages. We must base our understanding upon our behavior at its best, when we are free of selfishness and greed, of hunger and desire to profit at the expense of others. This way we can regenerate our wholeness and return to unity. Thus will we regain our understanding of how we are joined in a way that transcends the divisions that appear to us now as truth, as fact, as knowledge. We must be for giving, and against taking for ourselves at the expense of those who are weaker or poorer. Our word must be the One that joins us together as human beings, the Love which will not allow us to exploit others. Our Word must have the gravity that brings together and unifies.

We have the capacity to develop an integrated worldview that brings human beings together to perform our work. This in no way supposes we will suddenly give up our cultural and personal diversity and by some means become alike. As it is in the cosmos, in the earth, and within our own beings, diversity is to be welcomed, celebrated, and encouraged. We need our differences, for there must be some kind of tension in order for movement and growth to continue. But we do not need greed or war. There is enough for everyone if we willl take the time to rectify and equalize the flow of goods and services across the planet and make sure all are provided for.

We must live together and share what we have and live within our means on the one hand, while making certain that all are provided for according to their capacities and needs on the other. There is enough for everyone in the world. But there is never enough for the greedy, who profit from human suffering. It is time we provided all with an alternative approach to living and dying, a means of bringing the elements together for the betterment of all human beings. We must insure that people have food, shelter, and their basic needs fulfilled. After that it's up to them to progress into an expanded and deeper unity in the heart of the planetary mind.

No single ideology is enough. Democracy, Communism, Socialism, Capitalism—all must be drawn upon in differing ways depending on the people and the situation where they are applied. All of these depend solely upon the word that lives in us to exist. No religion will overcome the differences bred in misperception and propagated in the Word. All modern views emerged from a shared understanding that predates all pre-set forms. This understanding must supercede all the fragmented and derivative, broken down and divisive views to the contrary.

With love, through the word, by virtue of the gravity inherent in our awareness, we will achieve a more balanced and dynamic equilibrium some day if we so choose. Let us gather ourselves together once more, we human beings, and renew our union. Let us put an end to greed, and insure that all the goods and services are distributed in an equalized way, unimpeded by the power that divides and breaks down. It's this, or greed will put an end to all of us. The imbalances in the human system must be rectified if we are to avoid disaster, disillusionment and extinction.

Our awareness will be illuminated by the Living Word, our world elevated to a global state of union with love. Our minds will be clear again, as it was in the beginning, as we find the source of the strange attractors of gravity that can keep us together in peace.

Hyperconsciousness

In the realm of computing there exist formats called hypertext and hypermedia, parallel processing and multitasking. In these types of operating systems all the component elements are interconnected and cross-referenced so as to make many things happen at the same time. In a multiplex fashion, such formats make identifying relationships between the elements easy.

In the Universal Mind this occurs naturally. All the elements from the beginning of the universe are related and connected in subtle and mysterious ways. Physicists have determined that any two photons that have been in contact with each other at any given point in space-time will be related forever. Whatever happens to the one of them will simultaneously influence the other. How can this be? Such a situation defies logic and appears to violate the laws of physics. It does not matter how far apart the packets of energy (photons and the quantum quarks) are—they are still connected. By what? No one seems to know. "As above, so below," the old saying goes, and as in the universe and planet, so it is within us.

We can assume for now that, within our own minds, all things are connected by the movement of electrons and ionized chemical compounds that propagate the impulses and patterns of activity we discern as thoughts. Hyperconsciousness is thus an ongoing integrative function operating within the human neural systems of awareness. It is a state of macro/micro cosmic integration whereby the inner and outer realms, instinct, emotion, thought, behavior and creativity are connected with one another. Through this connection they become coherent in such a way as to clarify the elements of thought, and bring us in tune with the universal processes of creation.

The electrochemical storms of creativity and vision within our minds are analogous to the formation of stars and galaxies. In this living universe in which we are embedded, all things are in fact joined in the process of creation, whether we sense, perceive, and recognize it or not. When a state of awareness is reached where this becomes evident and apparent, one enters into hyperconsciousness and sees the interrelatedness of all things. One sees that, indeed, there are "not two."

Two is not twice as much as one, but one divided. Our universe is based upon this tendency to continually divide. Yet, it is still one, still unified, still integrated and all things are connected. Those who never see this will gradually come to know only disintegration, incoherence, and the sense of mortality upon which our concepts of death are predicated. Those who, on the other hand, achieve an enhanced state of awareness, regardless of the means of its initiation, will gain a sense of the immortal, the infinite, the universal—"the universe in a grain of sand, and all time in a wildflower." Those who find freedom will see how connected all things are, how creation is joined together as a totally interconnected experience.

Hyperconsciousness sets us free of the limits of self. It enables us to craft vehicles of sound which provide us a means whereby to roam the constellations of thought. It allows us to be inspired by the beauty, the joy, the unity of heaven and earth, stones, water and wind. It is the celestial fire of life which inhabits our beings and is forever returning, forever seeking itself, forever whole, undivided, joined together as one, not two.

Not Two

Senstang, the third Zen Patriarch said that, "whenever you are in doubt, say, not two." As mentioned earlier, even Einstein understood the basic problem with our limited sensory system and perceptual processing. Because each of our senses is tuned to specific elements and bandwidths of the electromagnetic spectrum and natural environment— sight to light, hearing to sound, taste to chemical composition, smell to molecular configuration, and touch to temperature, pressure, humidity, etc.— there seem to be clear, clean divisions between what we sense, perceive, and recognize as the world we live in.

But there again one runs into the problem basic to all human awareness as expressed in the hundreds of languages that exist today. Rather than being a means of shedding light, of illuminating the inner recesses of our experience, language acts as a filtering system that determines what is excluded from our basic sensibility. The way we think and speak divides the world into convenient, culture-bound categories that separate rather than join things together.

If this were not so, and we lived in a totally singular unity, spoke a universal language, the world would look very different, and we might not so easily be able to discern where we ought, and ought not to be. We might not see objects as solid, cliffs as drop-offs, or understand the differences between what is beneficial and what is not. We would also be free of the limiting visions imposed on our awareness by our cultures, religions and nations. Thus it is that language acts to both limit and enhance our survival. It is a tool, the technology of our imagination, a figurative gift from the gods. In fact, the ancient language of Sanskrit, from which English is descended, is called the "language of the gods."

Language provides us with a means of defining and relating to the world around us. However, it also has inherent in its nature the potential for becoming a sort of substance to which we attach our identity. Words, as they exist in the mind, act as magnets that can either attract or repel. Around the "dust" that acts as a nuclear gathering point, neurologically equivalent experience gathers, gradually clouding the matter, rendering the true nature of original experience opaque. We begin to gradually identify with the screen rather than the source of what is projected. We see ourselves as reflections of the multiplicity of terms and definitions rather than their generators. Thus we are broken into pieces: families, states, nations, races, religions. All are partial in their ability to represent human experience.

We store up the years as memories and believe they are us. But the fact is that memory is inexact, selective, and fuzzy. It is doubtful, for instance, that you can remember what you had for breakfast or wore on you tenth birthday unless something happened of note, something exceptional and unusual which allowed those details to be fixed in your mind. What we don't know, we tend to imagine or forget.

Every perspective provides a different viewpoint. This is why it can be so frustrating for the police when they try to reconstruct an accident or crime and have to piece the situation together from a variety of perspectives. Even though everyone saw what appeared to be exactly the same thing, each selected from the scene only those aspects of importance as they saw it. Yet, there was only a singular incident being reported! Not two.

The Art of Forgetting

Sometimes you must be willing to go out of your mind. The individual mind is infused with the intelligence of the Universal Mind, but from the moment we're born, this intelligence is being buried within the experience of the individual self, and a sense of separateness grows. We learn to name the world around ourselves, to recognize what we sense and perceive within the space we inhabit. We must give it definition in order to create the familiarity that brings order to the swirling chaos of experience as it occurs for the infant.

The problem with defining the world is that we eventually learn what to screen out, eliminate, ignore and become unaware of. Thus we become ever more unconscious as we age. Another interesting phenomenon concerns the temporal displacement caused by the process of recognition. It takes about three hundredths of a second for an incoming signal, a raw input into our sensory system, to go through the process of making a sensory impression, to initiate our perceiving the nature of the impression in relation to ourselves, and to recognize the meaning of that relationship. By the time we recognize what's happened, it's already over! We are living in the past! We lose our innocence in the process of becoming ourselves! The act of constructing an identity creates a prison for our soul. No matter how it howls to get out, we keep it in well-defined chains and hope it will remain asleep. What a surprise when it rises to the surface and says, "let me wake up."

When I was young man, with pretensions of becoming a great poet, I asked my poetry teacher, James Dickey, what I needed to do. He said, "You have to go back to the caves and imagine what it was like to lie there on your back in the dim light painting pictures on the stone, then rise and go out to become the first man, speaking the first word, on the first day—that's where poetry begins." I understood I'd have to forget all I'd ever learned in order to make that one leap backwards in time, into the primal intelligence which is the foundation of all our modern varieties.

Zen Roshi wrote about the need to have a "Zen mind, beginner's mind" in order to forget the conditioned responses through which we relate to our experience. We must be willing to go out of our minds on purpose. We must return to the clarity and purity of an infant's innocence, the first moment of awareness, before the names, memories, and experiences of the individual self took over our frame of reference. We must go back to the time before the individual mind experienced the accretion of psychological dust and debris around the polarized points of reference related to experience. In this way we can become aware of how our individual identity is being distorted to fit society's frame of reference, ideas, and definitions.

Our experience does not belong to us. Odd thought that. We are each a passing thought in the infinite and universal mind of the cosmos. You could say, if words were not so limiting, that we are all one of the means by which the power of creation experiences the infinite diversity of being. The intelligence which lives within us, which keeps our hearts beating, our breath going in and out against all the odds and forces of resistance in nature, is absolutely and totally connected to, within, and throughout all the elements and forces in the universe. There is only one soul, shared by all that exists.

We are not separate from the power of creation. We are joined in creation. The great circle of life is whole, and we are whole. But in our remembering who we are, we forget what we truly are. Sometimes, to be free, innocent, pure, and clear so that our experience again becomes transparent, so that we can again see the one source of life, we must also remember to forget, and be willing to go out of our minds.

This is the art of forgetting.

Mind As Metaphor

When we consider the possibility of a Planetary Mind, we must remember that this too is but a tool, a symbol, a metaphor. We could speak, as Carlos Castenada did, of "the eagle's gift" or of "God" or Allah, or Crom, or Brahmn, or of any other number of conceptually convenient cognitive tags that represent the unbounded, undefinable, unmanifest, unknowable power that is evident without being apparent. The Tao Te Ching says, "for lack of better name we can call it 'Great'." We know it exists, but we cannot know what it is. "The way that can be spoken of is not the true way." The laws of systems theory indicate that it is not possible for a given specific component of a sub-system to be aware of, to know the nature of, or to describe the greater system within which it operates.

The wholeness of the universe is beyond knowing. It can only be experienced. Knowledge will never take us anywhere but further into the division of the One into the infinite fragments that emerge from the unified singularity. We can be aware of this, but can never define it.

Words are not things, nor do they define things. They are but cognitive tags for electrochemical events within our cerebral cortex. If we are focusing our curiosity on the words that are aftereffects of experience, we are lost in the past. If we base our hopes on imagining the future, we are lost in the world of the dreamer. To take action we must be centered in this moment, in the complete experience of the life we contain.

Jesus commented on this. When asked by his disciples about the laws in the Jewish holy books which a man seemed to have violated in order to save his ass from a hole in the ground, he said that what is written is "the dead letter of the law." As soon as we start the name game, we kill the immediacy of life.

If we base our identity upon the named, defined, and known, then we limit and divide ourselves thereby. This destroys the circle of life and breaks it into pieces. We are left feeling alone, alienated, separate, and apart from our creator. We must focus on the disturbing point of reference and identity that has no qualities and characteristics, and therefore no definition or personality.

In Hinduism the metaphor used is that of Brahmn. This is a metaphor that represents what contains and is contained by all that exists. It is too much for us to know, but we contain enough of it to be aware that it is. What it is. "Thou art that that thou art." This construct is made manifest in the human realms as the trinity of the Hindu cosmology, Brahma, Vishnu, and Shiva, the creator, preserver, and destroyer elements of being. It is further represented in the pantheon of gods, goddesses, and metaphysical beings of that belief system.

One would need to take, as with any set of metaphysical constructs—religion—a lifetime to learn the depth and complexity of this view. But suffice it here to say that I learned my lesson in my youth when studying yoga with some of the gurus from India. My jhana yoga teacher—the yoga of knowledge, of scriptures—told me, when I asked him why I had to read and recite the lessons, sutras, and scriptures over and over that, "what you will learn from the books is how to close them."

Mind is but a metaphor, as, in a sense, are we. We are vaporous glyphs, biological symbols, passing energies in formation, the expressions of universal intelligence and the power of creation. What craft shall we use to fly beyond the limits of our temporal beings, to access what actually is, to bring harmony and peace to our families, our nations, our world, and ourselves? We can rise from the ashes of material existence and travel the cosmos if we try.

We can generate wholeness, be representations—metaphors—of the one from which the multitudes come forth. First, we unify ourselves. The rest of the universe will follow.

Hologenics

This book focuses on how to develop an enhanced world view (holos), a new approach (genic) to living and dying in the twenty-first century which will enable us to fill the moral vacuum at the heart of the world, the black hole into which our future pours. How are we to bring forth the Universal Mind within each person? How are we to get over the materialism and limiting ideas upon which the illusions of separateness and death are built and develop our own planetary mind? What means are we to use to regenerate our wholeness, to heal the great circle of life, to bring peace within ourselves, and the world we live in?

It is the process of Hologenics that ties all the information herein together: this is an alternative approach to living and dying in the twenty-first century. The faulty psychological framework in which we are mired can be restructured so as to be a multi-tiered system that describes mind at all systemic levels, from the quantum sub-atomic domains, to the molecular, chemical, personal, communal, national, planetary, and universal points of view. The systemic nature of the physical realms is easily expressed from the quark to the photon, sub-atomic particles, atomic parts, molecular, inorganic and organic chemical domains, cellular, biological, ecological, global, solar, galactic and cosmic spaces.

It is through the systemic approach embodied in Hologenics that we can achieve expanded sensory perception, enhanced cognitive awareness, hyperconsciousness, and immortality. By integrating our beings we become whole, we give rise to wholeness, and improve ourselves, and the world around us. We are the human beings, and we are joined in this journey. It is only the illusion of separation imposed by sensory limitation and social conditioning that imprisons us in primitive nation-states, with a fragmented identity, no center, no truly moral heart, alienated, divided. We are at odds with others, the environment, and ourselves. Hologenics integrates our system and gives rise to the life that is whole.

It is in the best interests of religions, governments, corporations, and historic cultures to keep humanity in the dark, the circle broken, the human beings apart. We are moving into the photonic age. The electronic age is already coming to a close, as the atomic and industrial ages did before it.

Light is spectral, not digital alone, as only the computing, information processing, and signaling systems are necessarily binary. Consciousness is multiple and subtly varied. This is why computers cannot be conscious. The brain is a broad band multiplex operating system of parallel harmonic channels working at the same time in many combinations of frequency, amplitude, loudness and hue, saturation, intensity. This means there are many complex processing systems working together at the same time. Every nerve in our body has a neuron at the other end, and these are all connected to one another directly or indirectly. By releasing ourselves from the limits of individualism, materialism, and egoism, we are enabled to experience this inherent unity within. We can discover the means of overcoming the fear of being-without, of loss, of emptiness, the illusion of death, the terminal sensibility.

When this is done, the individual mind is cleared of all the chaff and dust that distort the lenses of perception. The cloudy accretions, the dark matter and dust are blown away, burned out, and baked off. The dusty haze that prevents us from truly seeing as participants in creation is gone. One can then turn one's full power, attention, and focus on how to best express this altered consciousness effortlessly, to use the gravity of the word of love to bring human beings together. How is this to be brought about? Hologenics is the method. The Living Word, as it has been in the form of our oral traditions, is the means.

Hologenics clarifies the matter. It involves being conscious in everything we do, awake, aware, whole, complete. Buddhists call it "right mindfulness." We are the body of the immortal power of creation, vessels through which awareness moves, in which it lives, by which it becomes full and unified. We must breathe, drink, eat, reproduce, work, care, speak, think, and be human with full understanding of the nature of the relationships between the elements of the systems that comprise us. This involves learning to be clear, pure, innocent, and able to come to rest, to see, to be whole. The first step in this process is to read works such as this that illuminate the way.

After that a host of means exist in part, whereby one might find one's way back to the original points of experience around which memories are wrapped. Layer after layer of experiences are gathered and deposited from the beginning. Looking out through these layers, the world we see is often quite different from the world that actually is.

Any means that enables us to return to the beginning of experience is viable and useful.

Numerous methods exist whereby one can facilitate the hologenic process, bring about systemic reform through contemplative activity, and tear away the gauze that veils our vision of creation and our part in it. Hologenics involves becoming systemically aware, completely awake, and able to participate in life without exertion, to take part without taking action, to be without limit. Any method will do for a start, for in the end they all lead to the same place—now, here.

Before enlightenment you must cut wood and carry water. After enlightenment you must cut wood and carry water.

Singularity

"Once there was a pilgrim who followed a path to the top of a mountain. When she turned around and looked back, she saw there was no path, no mountain, no pilgrim." When we look around, we see what appears to others. But in fact there is no other. As long as there is an other, there is division. As long as there is division, one can feel separated, alienated, fragmented, and ultimately alone. But this is an illusion, an effect generated by our limited senses, perceptions, and ideas about the meaning of our being here now.

It is undeniable that we are individuals, with our unique complement of genetic inheritance, personal, familial, and social conditioning, language, culture, and values, attitudes, and beliefs. But these are only a part of the whole, the bigger picture.

The Universal Mind exists in singularity. It is the One. There are not two. There is no other. This in no way means that this one does not have an infinite diversity, an array of qualities, forms, and characteristics which can be recognized and appreciated for their distinctive qualities. It is just that we cannot remain forever caught up in the illusion of separation if we are to get beyond ourselves, forget the past, let loose of that which binds, holds, and imprisons us, and extend our identity in the greater whole, the universe, and immortality.

Being whole is a singular business. The universe we inhabit emerged from singularity. Our galaxy has, at its heart, a black hole, a powerful concentration of energy and matter. From this emptiness, nothing escapes until the pressures build to the point that it explodes and a new star system is born. Something analogous to a black hole exists in the center of our beings as well.

Everything falls into that pure emptiness as it returns to the complement of being, or non-being. The universe is emptiness primarily, and the wisps of atoms, molecules and chemicals that float about at various speeds and in various concentrations have energy, mass, density, frequency, amplitude, loudness, hue, saturation, intensity. However, these are but a few of the multitude of characteristics and qualities. The emptiness is given meaning by the intelligence that permeates and perceives all being and non-being alike.

When we identify with this all-embracing intelligence, we are accepting everything that exists. It is in the heart of all, and simultaneously at the most distant, furthest reaches and edges of the universe. We exist in a bubble of space and time, and the primary intelligence of universal being, forever singular, is forever seeking itself, searching out means and mediums of self-recognition and expression. We are a most fortunate sort of entity, in that we are able to look across the seas of time and space. We look out across infinity itself and can there see ourselves as the source and the result of what may be fifteen billion years of tenuous development, growth, evolution, and change.

The flux we contain, the sense of uncertainty, the indeterminate quality of being, even the notion that we live, and that our bodies eventually expire, are all the norm, the shared truth. But in the singular view there is nothing eternal or universal, nothing to worship or fear. There is only the potential for intelligence and awareness and being. When we accept this, we can then come to know what love truly means. It is the union of self and other, the joining of all and nothing. We are not alone, cannot be alone, and loneliness is impossible when the identity is whole. Yet, we are singular, and within our beings contain all others. It is our function then to realize our potential for expanded awareness.

Societies have existed for many thousands of years with their primary intent being to restrain the population, hide these truths, and prevent the unmasking of the falsehood underlying imposed, arbitrary limitations. As such, most socially approved views, most norms, exist as general possibilities rather than absolute conditions. The last time we had all things in common was many tens of thousands of years ago. What we have today is a corruption of our original shared understanding rooted in nature and instinct.

When we do not understand this, there is always the shadow of what we have become, always the hidden self, waiting somewhere to come forth and shatter the illusion of separation. It forever awaits its chance to rise and shake off the accumulated dust of the eons and sing out of how we are all together, and how any sense of identity that does not embrace the All is a denial of the truth, and of the nature of being. It is a refusal of our inherited intelligence, which is nothing more or less than that of the universal mind, the power of creation, the awareness of being a unified self with a planetary mind.

Once we attain our wholeness, we become ever more permeable, transparent, porous, empty reflections of the universe. In this transparent universe, everything flows and moves without impedance, without meeting resistance, free of charge, holding onto nothing, ready to forever be and remain immortal.

True freedom is to be without form, without definition or limit, singular and multiple at once. Nothing is anything until we make something of it, until we capture it in our memories, our thoughts, dreams, words, and separate definition of self. Until that moment it's all free and empty, infinite, immortal, changeless and yet perpetually changing. This is the experience of pure being, of transcendent intelligence that is beyond life and death, self and other, and all paradox. It cannot be described or it disappears. We know it exists, but we cannot speak of it without losing sight of it. It cannot be defined without killing it, and yet it escapes definition and cannot cease to be. This is who we truly are: luminescent beings, organic prisms in which light collects, gathers itself, and shines through as it passes from one state into another. We are light that is dreaming of seeing itself. Earth is a passing thought in the mind of the universe, and we are from the beginning the pure thoughts of the planetary mind.

Nets of Infinite Light

One ancient belief system viewed the creator of the universe as a great spider, and saw all things as the result of the infinite web spun by it. Wherever the threads of the web met, there gathered substance that gave rise to the elemental and organic forms of the universe, from dark to light, from simple to complex, from micro to macro. This is a beautiful conception, for it illustrates the nature of our beings. We live in the networks of infinite light that are the webs of being that form the universe within which we human beings exist.

The interconnections of life are evident in everything around us. Merely looking with the eyes of a child upon the web of a spider indicates the delicacy, intricacy, and beauty of things. We are all connected in a web of gossamer fineness combined with the strength of steel. We humans are electric walking mud puddles, water's way of moving around the web-work that is our world.

We can see only a minuscule portion of the nets, the webs, the system of lights wherein we glow, rise and fall, come and go. With our technology we have become aware of just how broad the spectrum is, and yet still have not come to be aware of any but the grosser aspects of its fullness. There are still powers and energies unknown to us, but accessible when we are at rest, at peace, still and undistracted by the movement of our individual egos and sense of self.

We cannot stop or overcome the rise and fall of phenomena. Transformation and transition are ongoing, both within and beyond us. But we can learn to be still, listen to ourselves breathe, feel our hearts beat and the blood moving through our veins, and watch the beautiful coming and goings of awareness in ourselves, and thus be immersed in the webs of infinite light that are the singing strings of the universe as it is manifest in us.

We can achieve unity, discover our transcendent nature as human beings, get past the limits that define and imprison us in self, nation, religion, race, etc. Then we are free to forget ourselves, travel freely through the constellations of thought, understand the symbolic nature of experience, and achieve singularity.

The nets of infinite light are our home, our beings, our source, and our destiny. All we need to do is realize that we are already whole and free, liberated, illuminated, enlightened, and able to effortlessly cut wood and carry water as empty and full as the universe, as simple as a child watching the spider at work.

Systems Meditation

Hologenics does not result in the end in peace. It begins in peace. It is based on a systemic view wherein all things are harmoniously interconnected. It is realized through exercises designed to bring the human being into the numinous realm of pure awareness wherein the transcendent being is the chief of operations. Matter or soul drives us. That's our singular choice. We can exert control over what drives us through proper exercise of the mind and body.

Various exercises have been used in numerous forms by human beings for ages, and continue to be the basis for the realization of human potentials among many peoples today. But we of the modern, particularly the English speaking, world have yet to translate these ancient activities and methods into a form we can most universally utilize. Thus one of the purposes of hologenics is to accomplish this task and convey to today's human beings what they need to know to make the transition into the unified field of awareness emerging in the twenty-first century.

We were once one in nature due to the universality of early earth environments. We shared instincts, ways of communicating, the basics of human life. We are now able to return to the One in culture due to the proliferation of the global telecommunications media. The process of globalization is bringing us back together, like it or not.

Let us remember that we are, each of us, a metaphor, a symbol, a character in a genetic transcription, a note in a symphony, a word in the sentences uttered by the power of creation. We can thus, for convenience, look upon ourselves in a variety of ways. For the purposes of hologenic exercise we can view the body as a collection of seventy-two thousand tubes, channels, passageways, fibers, organic wires, or the like. Each of our twenty-four principle vertebrae is a switch for up to three thousand channels of information, connected to more than ten billion neurons with upwards of ten to the twenty-third power of connections between them!

Our brains are composed of three interactive systems; the mid-brain, the limbic system, and the outer cortex. The mid-brain handles our physical systems, senses, the ongoing work of maintenance and repair of the body, growth, etc. The limbic system handles our emotive experiences, the hormonal and chemical signals, the non-linguistic elements of our beings. The outer cortex is composed of six ascending layers of cells, each one more complex than the one below it, and deals with our perceptual, cognitive, and abstract information processing. The brain is sub-divided into many specialized parts and areas of intelligence, but it is not necessary to go into any further detail in order to engage in the integrative exercises to be described here. All that's necessary is to understand that the brain, nervous system, and body are all joined in a symphonic movement of enormous complexity and beauty individually. The combined activity of all human bodies in the world creates a super organism, humanity, which plays a role in nature as a whole, which is an integral part of the total environment of the planetary body.

We are joined, like it or not. As the poet, Robert Frost, noted, "People work together whether they work together or apart." We are part of a seamless whole. He also said, "good fences make good neighbors." As such, we must clarify our elements, become permeable, transparent, and open to the flow of energy that is the power of life, creation, and the cosmos. This is not a metaphysical construct or idea, but a very concrete fact. We must seek to realize these unions if we are to generate wholeness within and without, and become seers of the nets of infinite light that all together are the ties which bind us in perpetual union. Through the unity of systems we are brought back together. Therein we redefine our most basic relationships to one another, biological, family, community, and humanity in general. Defining our systems is thus essential in light of the need to integrate with unlike systems.

The first system of the body begins at the lips and ends at the anus physically, and deals with transforming foods into energy primarily. The second system is the reproductive tract. The third system deals with the transmutation of grosser solid substances into purified forms, and connects us to the subtler elements that the body can use for maintenance and to power our activities. The fourth system deals with respiration and transpiration of gases and fluids such as air, water, lymph, and so forth, specifically the movement of oxygen, hydrogen, nitrogen, blood plasma, and other elements within this elemental realm or domain. The fifth system consists of the expressive parts of our makeup, the endocrine glands and particularly speech and language. The sixth is that which regulates our hormonal and glandular elements as well as our powers of intuition and insight. The seventh is the integrated holism referred to most often as the spiritual domain.

Each of these systems is subdivided and interconnected with others, as well as acting as the basis for the energetic bodies of sensation, perception, emotion, thought and interactivity with the surroundings. Remember that this description is metaphorical, based upon material fact, but symbolic in nature—thus it has arisen and been utilized as the basis for numerous metaphysical constructs and systems over the ages.

In short order, the systems of meditation in each physical and energetic center are concerned with food, sex, attachments to people, places, and things, love, the word, knowledge and intuition, and spirituality. Each dimension of our whole being must be considered and brought into harmony in order for us to achieve a hologenic being and experience the expansion of awareness. This expanded awareness leads to the realization and fulfillment of our human potentials as integrated individuals, families, communities, and so on.

Our bodies therefore reflect the order of the cosmos, while our social and cultural domains reflect the union of the earth and sky, water and wind in a supernatural domain of harmonic human organization, which was achieved in nature in those fortunate cultures that achieved dynamic equilibrium in relation to their surroundings. We have yet to see a situation arise in which a globalized civilization can achieve balance among most human groups in the same way that individual cultures can.

There are many varieties of, and variations upon, this basic model of how to approach our awakening. It all begins with such simple things as reading a few words on the subject in one or another book, language or tradition. One can see this in the Hindu Gitas, the Moslem Koran, the Judaic Kabbalah, the Christian Bible or the Communist Manifesto. Religions are not, in and of themselves, any more than metaphorical systems. Reading them is not enough, and is in fact meaningless without an attendant practice that develops into an integrated lifestyle. Context is everything.

For the purposes of this book we can simply call this practice of hologenic expansion of mental awareness Systems Meditation. We each seek out various forms that suit us in order to find a way to achieve our fullest development. As the Zen koan noted earlier says: "Before enlightenment you must cut wood and carry water. And after enlightenment you must cut wood and carry water." Understanding this is the key to finally achieving union and realizing our true nature as transcendent beings.

This view begins in peace, in starting from a point of rest, a singular focus, and in letting that singularity expand into all the various systems of one's being. We realize that all we experience are transitional states and perpetual flux. At the same time, all we know originates in the singularity in the core of creation. Realizing this leads to instant liberation, and a return to the place of rest in the heavens, on earth, within ourselves, from which everything comes.

Final Symbiosis

We all work together, whether we work together or apart, as noted previously in reference to the Frost poem. This is a deeper and more profound statement than it appears to be on the surface. "All things work together for good for those who love God," Timothy, a disciple of Jesus, said. These two writers, two thousand years apart in time, ten thousand miles apart in space, still work together to point out for us that the universe is moving along quite nicely and is open for our viewing if we can but forget what we are looking for in order to see what is actually there.

The intelligence of creation is evident, even if not always readily apparent, from the quark to the quasar. Everything works together in a harmonic fashion. When we are able to shed our limited ego identity and identify ourselves with this immortal power that permeates all that exists, we become likewise beyond limit. We are able to die to the world while still alive. We can give up our boundaries, attachment to appearances, people, places, and things, feelings and thoughts, and even our most deeply held beliefs. Our holding to the appearance of things is nothing more or less than a sort of "spiritual materialism," as Trungpa Rimpoche called this sort of possessiveness. Whether ethereal or not, identifying with limitation binds us in illusory states of existence.

The intelligence of the universal mind is forever returning to itself, flowing through, beyond, and into the source of all being, seeking itself. Our planet reaches into the cosmos at the speed of light and seeks other conscious planets. This understanding both affirms that creation is a symbiotic, interconnected process, and confirms that no matter how many parts it divides itself into, how great or small these parts are, it is still a singular intelligence without definite shape, form, definition, bounds, or limits. As we breathe, so does the whole sky. The fires of distant stars go into and out of the cores of their beginnings and ends, just as does the warm breath that enters and leaves us and assures us that we exist—at least for a while. It may appear that we are divided, but in fact we are made of one another; we live within each other. The light of life moves through us and pauses, lives in all of us at the same time as our shared soul.

We are the human beings here on the earth. We are a form of order piling up against the edges of eternity like musical waves against the shores of chaos. The mighty tides of life rise and fall, go in and out, come and go, always clearly there, but always beyond us as well. We are not in control, and can never be. We are participants in the universal process of creation. We are all symbiotic as we live, like it or not. There is no way to be apart from the whole but to be ignorant, asleep, and unwilling to regain the awareness and innocence that are our inheritance. This is the final symbiosis, therefore, the culminating union the soul longs to experience.

Buddha meditated for many years and concluded that there is a law of dependent arising, and a doctrine of insubstantiality. All things depend for their nature upon the conditions within which they arise. All things are in flux. Therefore there is nothing that is either permanent or universal in nature. As such the source of human suffering is to not realize that everything we are exists at this moment. We can thus be free of desire or want, and realize our potential. When this occurs, we are able to live fully, free of suffering, pain, fear, doubt, and be completely centered on this moment of bliss that is forever available.

Give up and receive. Lose to gain. Forget to know. Die in order to live. Such paradoxes and contradictions are true. Reason will not help us understand them. Experience will. Maturity will not bring them about. Being as a child insures the fullness of being. These messages have been among us living in the words of love and life among all peoples and times and places. They can only be denied with great effort, and to do so will put one in peril of losing one's immortality. True understanding will come to us while we are alive if we let it. Or it will take us when we are transformed and return to our heavenly state as our bodies drop away.

What has been said here is nothing new. Only the outer form is. The ideas, whether of the shaman, of hologenics, of the bards, singers, sorcerers, or whatever, are all a shared legacy which has been with us since the word came to life. Those who convey this are our saviors and saints, our lovers and friends. They are us, and we are them. Awaken now.

VI

The Teachings of One Wolf

I WAS TALKING WITH ONE OF MY OLD CHEROKEE TEACHERS, a man of the same medicine clans my family was part of, and he told me I was chosen to convey to others his message about what is past, and passing, and to come. This is what he said:

In the beginning I was but one, unified, at rest for eternity, silent, peaceful, in the heart and at the edges at once, perfect, complete. Then from something silent the vision emerged and the song, first man and first woman, who gave rise to the grandmother earth and grandfather sky, and the Word came among the human beings to give them the memory of creation, and the medicine people and chief speakers and leaders and makers gave it form and definition and preserved it among the generations. It was forty or fifty thousand orbits around the sun ago, and the singularity at the heart of the galactic being poured forth its light and music, that gives birth to new suns and worlds, shapes the space, forming from the emptiness the dance of cosmos, the Word of life, the light which joins the star people in their motions of dust, sending the rays of radiant power into the distant reaches of the circle of life. It was then I came into the world, into the human beings, and took the form of the people so as to remember for them our origins and the good red way. Into the clay and the turquoise, into the water and corn, into the winds and into the fire, without beginning or end, joining the elements in the continuing prayers and chants of creation in formation.

In the olden times, when we were all of one people and Word, when we were joined in the unity of nature and the life within it of the People, the sacred circle of all things was whole. The natural people, the first people, the old ones who communed with the plants and animals, the sacred elements and their movements through the directions, are still here, still living among

140

the materialists in the shadows of the stupendous and beastly material complex of national and international corporate power. We have maintained our integrity, sustained our invisibility, our transparent spirits of clear water, our sacred fires, the living earth, and pure air along with the old powers and songs which have allowed us to conceal ourselves, change forms as need be, and enter into the immaterial realms effortlessly so as to benefit the human beings and provide useful direction.

With the plants and stones, with the animals and the powers of the ancestors, we entered into union, entered into the spiritual world where all is power, where the only real battles are, where the dreams are born, and where we seek the answers of the ancients for the problems which perplex us. We of the medicine clans, the singers of the dawn, the travelers in the night, the warriors of the spirit who know the attractive power of the Word, of love, of gravity, have continued our work through the ages of maintaining the clarity of our shared vision, and have sustained the circle of life, despite the various ways and means of life the people have learned in order to survive.

Five hundred years ago we came before the chiefs, elders, clan mothers and people, and told them the white man was like the grass, that there would always be more of them, and that they would eventually spread us like dust on the wind. But they have no love of the mother in the earth, and would also gradually exhaust her until she could give them no more. Then, when they were on their knees in their streets, praying to their god to come save them, the First People, the Ani Keetowah Tsragi, would return to show them how to live, and what is today known as the Cherokee Nation would return.

Now we come forth again with such songs as this: Long ago, after our differentiation into the countless divisions and factions, after we had wandered into all the world and settled into our selected environs, developed our various languages and ways of life, we began to see ourselves as separated from the primal union, as unique, as different, and the old prayers in the original tongue were translated into such diverse forms as to lose much of their unity and power for those whose beings were not conceived before the beginning of our kind in the great spirit which contains and is contained by all. Still we of the circle, the first people, maintained our prayers and chants, our incantations and spells, our knowledge of that which cannot be known, but can only be experienced in a being that is clear and free of the filtering of the split tongues.

Today we continue in our work of keeping the circle whole, despite all that has been done to erode its power and integrity. We have left our pictures on the stones, left our songs in the tongues, left our signatures in the talking leaves so that we might never forget ourselves and lose the way given to us by the power of creation. We have risen and fallen over the ages, been born and died among the divided peoples of the world, but have retained our shared connection to the natural world, while also understanding the need for the people to develop fully in the material realms so as to realize our potentials as human beings. Now it is again time for us to join together the spiritual and the material, the natural and the mechanical, the elemental and the living, inorganic and organic, and recreate civilization, provide the means for global unity and cultural integrity to continue into the next cycle of human development. It will be costly, but the ordination of those who administer the healing is older than memory, and will set them loose to carry us over and into what is to come.

Thus it is that I came to live my life, to heed the advice of the clan mothers with whom I am acquainted, who have appointed me singer and keeper of the memory of the People, tender of the medicine fire, that the time is very near for full surrender to the power I and all my relations continue to serve and express. All the writing and teaching, the travels and relationships, are the lessons of my inheritance, my obligation to discern, unravel, and fulfill. For this we were chosen before the beginning, when the circle formed in the center of being which gave expression, through the medicine people, to the knowledge of creation in this world. The dimensions and seas of time and space I have crossed from the emergence of the Pink Clan Ray from First Person, from First Man and First Woman, from the grandfather and grandmother of our kind are great, yet I remain still in this world unperturbed from when the Word arrived among the First People, and I have lived in, with, and beyond them from the start.

It is our task in this coming time to release our people from attachments to persons and places and things, to surrender fully to the realized potential of our being an expression of the healing medicine of the circle of the earth and of the Wolf Clan. This change has begun. There is, according to the mothers, no more than a couple of decades left before we must come forth and deliver our news of the way of the circle among all peoples, to give birth to the emerging civilization which will unify the natural and material worlds, the singular First People with the divided multiple Moderns. Many great shifts in power, borders, and human identity will occur. There will be a loss of one-third to one-half of all that lives in our world. The air, the earth, the water, and the fires we are tending will come alive to illuminate and unify the human beings for generations to come at the same time as they consume all that resist our union. According to the old calendars this age is coming to an end as population outstrips food resources, as the energy of petroleum is sucked dry, as the very earth buckles beneath the weight of the material civilization.

There will be a massive collapse of the world economy, while at the same time the global telecommunications system will be completed. All peoples in developed lands who are not implanted with the bio chip that contains their records, accounts, worth, and social value will be excluded from the system initially—but the First People will not use or need these, as we have other means by which we will sustain our union and our beings. The marked ones will eventually be eliminated in a global conflict which arises after the emergence of the Great Witch Who Offers To Save who comes and takes power in the world of nations. Those of us chosen to remain will continue our work and keep the bodies and souls of the circle, and of our people, whole. I know at this juncture of my life that this is what I must focus on to be complete and empowered with the Word of Life that is Light and Song that is Love. I have received a clear signal that, if we divert any more time and energy into any other endeavors, it will result in distress within, and impede the equalized flow of energy through the systems. It is time to awaken to multi-modal, multiplex awareness, and to reflect the wholeness of the circle of life of the First People. For this reason I am making this declaration of intent to you. The clan mothers tell me that I, One Wolf, am to call on to my allies—the Bear, Snake, Wolf, Fox, the Longhairs, and their powers of transformation—and that I must share the medicine of my father who was a great and powerful hunter and warrior, and give my name to the work to be done now.

Once he told me all this, he left America and went to live and work among the Sammi peoples of Scandinavia, to help them translate their sacred traditions into modern tongues.

He also said that I am the flower of the seed of many peoples, of six kinds of northern Europeans, and two Indian peoples, and am the product of the ancient spirits of all my relations that taught me in the medicine ways. I am also the product of modern educational institutions and teachers who have trained me, qualified me, and provided means to accomplish the things I have described as a scholar, poet, writer, and teacher. Because of this heritage I am now ready to begin the healing work, prepared fully to give back to the human beings their lost and broken memories, to convey the teachings of One Wolf to those who are willing and able to listen.

For this reason I have written this book, and why I will now conclude it with the rest of our story.

Where Do We Come From?

According to current findings, somewhat controversial still, modern human beings first emerged out of Africa from a common ancestor about 200,000 years ago. Anthropologist Loren Eisley noted in his writings that human life only emerged on one continent and traveled to all the others. How did they get to the place we now call America? There are many modern ideas on this subject, constantly changing. Most focus on the Bering Land Bridge theory. The problem is that evidence is not consistent with this theory. There is evidence of human occupation or passage at sites in New England, Texas, the Great Lakes region, Brazil, Chile, and on the American Northwest coast that suggest humans arrived in the Americas long before the accepted date of 10,000 to 12,000 years ago.

In addition, the "facts" of Western sciences are the "myths" of the first people themselves. Our oral traditions are not always in agreement with scientific traditions. How are we, as unfamiliar as most of us are with the various stories of how the Human Beings developed into the First Peoples of what later became America, to resolve the conflicting evidence?

We must look at information from the Western scientific disciplines, from genetics, linguistics, anthropology, archaeology and geography. We must look as well at American Indian oral and literary traditions. Then we must use the planetary mind to integrate the apparent differences between what they each say into a holistic view of the many possible ways and means the Human Beings followed as they came to be the First Peoples of Turtle Island in the Americas. First, let's look at some stories.

The Creation Stories:

1. At first there was a tiny fireball. It exploded and cooled and expanded into the emptiness. From this came the stars, elements and the worlds. The earth was a rock with a molten core. Solar radiation interacted with the developing Earth and gave rise to the atmosphere and oceans. Out of the seas came the first life forms—single-celled creatures, multi-celled, then multi-cellular organisms, and eventually super-social organisms such as man. Such is the scientific view.

2. Without beginning God created the heavens and the Earth. There was silence on the face of the waters. God spoke and the word, "light," and the cosmos came into being. God then made the heavens and the earth, day and night, and all the inhabitants of our world. Then God created man, woman, and the children of God, and they were told to multiply and spread over the world. This is the Judaeo-Christian view.

3. At first there was only God. But God got so lonely he got all broke up, and he's been trying to find himself again ever since. So the children say.

4. God Kneph looked out over the universe he had made. It was empty. He got bored. He began to masturbate. He ejaculated and the cosmos came forth from him. The Earth was created and the God took some clay and made a pot. This was the first man. This is the view of the ancient Egyptians

5. Everything was still, a sea of silence. First Person woke up. Something moved. First Person's mouth opened and a sound came forth that made things happen. It took the form of First Woman. First Person's eyes opened and many lights poured forth and gathered into the form of First Man. These were the ancestors of the fires of heaven, and of the First People. First Person is the Creator of all things, whose source is uncertain, but whose nature is self-evident, containing and contained by all things. A shining light spread. First Person wanted to stand on something, so stepped on the sun, but it was too soft. Then First Person stepped onto the fertile Earth, and First Woman, in the form of the great mother Earth, was warm and welcomed First Person, and the light of the Sun. First Man came forth and went into her and from the union of First Person, in the form of First Man, with the First Woman Earth, came forth the elements, and all living things. First Man wanted to see what he looked like. So he took upon himself some bones, blood, flesh, and breath and became the First Human Being on Earth. But the First Human Being was still but one being, so it divided in two and became the Grandfather and Grandmother of the First People who then came to be Human Beings in the earth. Through the four worlds they came, from the worlds of stone, fire, air, and water. From these four worlds we came into this one, led by the trickster. We are the children of water and our beings are made of the elements which came together and started to walk around. In time we return to the elements and the directions, to the sky, the stones, the stars. This is how One Wolf sees the beginning.

These are a few stories of how everything began. There are stories here from science, the Bible, Egypt, Indian America, and a child. There are literally as many creation stories as there are peoples in the world. No one of them is any more right or wrong than any other. In fact, they may have all come from what Carl Jung called our "collective unconscious." Perhaps all these views spring from a collective memory of some sort derived from the genetic records. They are first expressed in dreams or reverie, interpreted in relation to the local environment, and given form in words. They were eventually formalized into myths, stories, legends, chants, rituals, and ceremonies specific to each community.

Claude Levi-Strauss, Simon Frazier, Joseph Campbell, and other mythologists have noted that the structural elements of each community's mythos share elements in common with others around the world. Levi-Strauss even proposed that myth has a basic unit called the "mytheme," analogous to the phoneme in spoken language, which is the basic building block of all mythos. From the mytheme, through the deep structures of language, our myths are then eventually formalized in the spoken and written forms, ending up as the established religions and scriptures of each community.

Every people has a story. Each person has a story. The stories we share define who we are, where we came from, what happens when we die, and where we have been and gone during our time in the world. There are stories for everything. The consistency of this global, oral and literary tradition suggests the psycho-spiritual traditions of the world's peoples emerge from common biological, psychological, experiential and spiritual roots.

The diversity inherent in the countless mythic traditions and renderings, though at times confusing, begins to expand in scope, take on a more defined shape, a more meaningful pattern, when we realize they are the primary sources of our understanding of, and within, a given community. We must thus be open to this diversity without feeling we have any need to surrender our own familial and cultural traditions. Acceptance of diversity and tolerance of ambiguity in an ever more complex world enriches our worldview: the more diversity, the greater our adaptability.

What we believe is what we see. Our communities develop in direct response to environmental and social demands. Our sensations emerge from, and our perceptions are shaped by, nature, in the same way our cognition and behavior are shaped by culture. Natural selection and cultural selection go hand and hand in shaping the human world and our civilizations. The beliefs, values, and attitudes we identify with as groups are preserved in a shared language and environment. They are passed on through the artistic, oral and literary traditions developed in each community.

In America we have come to approach the study of people from a variety of systemic perspectives—atomic, molecular, chemical, genetic, biological, social, cultural, linguistic. Each one developed to its current state over the last few hundred years, coming forth from the unique linguistic traditions of Western natural science. Our modern sciences tend to reduce the study of our unified being to a categorical imperative that shapes the body of knowledge that comes forth from each of the various disciplines. Each discipline has developed its own set of terms. But we must transcend these disciplinary boundaries. It is time to draw upon each of them together in the process of coming to our own conclusions about where the First Peoples of America came from, and how they came to be, and by what means they have come to live where they are.

The Great Circle of Life

The land provides all. It is our mother. She gives us our bodies, materials, and environments to inspire our creative impulses for developing survival habits and our social and cultural forms. From our interaction with this mother comes the artistic, spiritual, and oral traditions of each community. Each groups' unique crafts, music, visual designs and symbols, dances, stories, clothing, food, architecture and way of life develop in a unique manner. People are gradually transformed as they interact with one another and their surroundings to create from bone, wood, and stone those things needed to obtain and maintain supplies of food, shelter and clothing. Our hunting and gathering tools and methods, and the social and cultural forms most appropriate within their local environment, emerge out of settling down in one place.

The word provides the means of preserving the myths, legends, stories and other information about how things got to be the way they are. The psycho-spiritual traditions embodied in the various languages and belief systems specific to each identity group are the repository of the taboos, customs, traditions, rituals, ceremonies, and other normative knowledge that tells the community how to live in harmony with all things.

Experience is organized and interpreted by the individual and group. The purpose of remembering is to maintain group identity and integrity and to allow for both cultural continuity and environmental adaptation over time as need be. Language preserves, transmits and shapes our actions, feelings, and thoughts. It also provides us with terms of convenience that we can use to study the unique cultural heritage, social structure and political legacy of the many hundreds of varieties of our native communities throughout North America and the world.

Each community develops a specific creation or origin story in response to its subjective experience. We need to look at the variety of opinions and theories in the bodies of both endogenous and exogenous knowledge regarding how the indigenous peoples came to be in America in the first place. In the process we'll utilize, in addition to the stories from various oral traditions, some of the primary terms and ideas considered useful in the academic disciplines that study such matters. Such terms are common to anthropologists, archaeologists, linguists, and geneticists.

The Human Beings in the Americas are said by scientists to have come over the Bering Land Bridge mentioned earlier. But we must also consider what some of the native peoples say as well. They say the Original People and the Modern Peoples are not the same. The former adapt themselves to nature and rely on a spiritual world view which says that everything is alive and involved in intimate relationships with everything else. The latter shapes the environment to fit its ideas and bases its progress on materialism, the view that holds the world to be made of dead matter to be exploited and dominated.

The Kusan peoples of the southern Oregon coast say they were created of the blue clay off of Cape Arago, and have never been anywhere else. The Hopi people speak of migrations from a faraway place into the Americas, and then they tell of how they explored the whole continent. The Spokane people of eastern Washington say they came from the sun. The Navajo say they came into this world from the one before in the Four Corners area of the American southwest, and that they were the first people in the world, and that all other peoples migrated from America to elsewhere. This last theory is called the "American Genesis."

The scientists and social scientists suggest this can't be so, and proceed to tell us that all the peoples of America came from Siberia through an ice-free corridor 10-12,000 years ago. They came across what's called the "Bering Land Bridge" and proceeded south until they filled the continent. The problem is, as noted earlier, this supposed theory is in direct conflict with some of the scientific evidence.

There are a number of other related stories. There is one that says people spread through the world around the edges of the polar ice cap. This "circumpolar" theory is not readily accepted, but is of interest for its originality.

Thor Heyerdahl tested his hypotheses that the peoples of America could have come by reed boats from Egypt to Brazil, or in canoes from Polynesia to central or South America. The Polynesian voyaging canoe, the Hokulea, recently completed circumnavigating the Pacific Island groups to show their prehistoric ancestral and traditional mastery of ocean navigation. Their system was based on currents, clouds, stars, birds, and other signs, every bit as accurate for them as the sextants and compasses of later Anglo-European navigators.

I am told in my own family that some of my native American relations began their travels along the coastline, by sea, from northern Africa to India. Then they traveled down the Australonesian archipelago into Australia and Polynesia. From the south Pacific they ventured to Hawaii, Easter Island, and thence to America's Yucatan peninsula. They went from the southern tropical climes and up the west coast as far as the Upper Columbia River Basin. They were a people with a portable technology and were willing to mingle with any others they came across along the way in order to strengthen and enrich their own genetic makeup.

The Mormon religion tells us they believe that the First Peoples in America are a lost tribe of Jews from the Semitic Mid-East! Their book of sacred lore tells of their leaving northern Africa, coming across the sea, engaging in internecine warfare, wiping out the light-skinned peoples, and falling from grace to become at last the "savages" in evidence when the Mormons got to Utah. Geneticists disproved this theory in 2002. Some origin stories are just plain wrong or made up.

A recent theory for which there appears to be significant evidence suggests that the peoples of the American northwest coast culture areas in fact came by foot and boat along the coastlines from northeastern China into the region. If indeed the oceans were bound in the ice caps, and the sea levels were lowered, there would have been a continental shelf upwards of one hundred miles wide to walk along. The islands of the south Pacific would have been much larger and more closely joined—perhaps this was the ancient land of Mu noted by the Chinese, or the homeland of Hawai'iki shared by the ancestors of the Polynesians.

And last, I must tell you what a Maori canoe carver told me about his own people. He said his people came from Sumeria or Mesapotamia across the Atlantic, landed in the Mississippi delta area and gave civilization to the Creek and Cherokee nations, traveled across the gulf to the Yucatan and civilized the Mayans and others of Mexico, Central, and South American nations, then carried their canoe overland to the Pacific where they proceeded to go to Easter Island, Hawai'i, and on to New Zealand, their modern homeland! How can this variety of stories render the truth about our origins?

There are many homelands. Pangaia, Atlantis, Mu, Hawaiiki, Africa. But there is no direct evidence accepted universally that could tell us for sure where we came from, and how we traveled along the great circle of life to where we are now. The oldest sites in South America outdate those in the north! On the other hand the Delaware tribe has an ideographic rendering that describes their migrations from—Siberia!

As you can see, the knowledge of our origins and migrations is not certain. No one was there to hand down a report directly to us. We only know what the stones and bones and stories say, and they are modestly quiet, communicating only in vague whispers of our ancestors and their ways. But the one thing they definitely indicate is that we are all related, and came from a common source, regardless of what we became. A recent study at the University of Florida of human genetics suggested that no one is more distantly related to any other than fiftieth cousin!

We know that all humans were once hunters and gatherers in the tropical and temperate climates. Humans discovered that fire could be used to kill parasites in animal flesh that would otherwise kill the unwary consumer. With the development of knowledge about how to make more efficient tools to hunt and trap game, the Original People were then free to roam north and south into less hospitable climates and around the world. True freedom! No fences, states or nations to get in the way. What remains today is the illusion of freedom, which comes only from the flock and their courts.

Let me take a moment to tell an old Cherokee story my grandmother told me about how the people got fire. This story is repeated throughout the world in various forms—as in the familiar story of Prometheus—attesting to the importance of its development and uses.

My elders say that a long time ago Possum had a beautiful tail with a lot of soft, warm fur. He'd sashay through the forest all night showing it off and telling everyone what a wonderful creature he was for having such a tail. One morning Possum was sleeping. He heard a lot of noise and chattering coming from the brush. It kept him awake. He decided to go see what it was. He found a group of Human Beings all huddled together in a pile, miserable in the cold. Possum had noticed that the world was getting a little colder, and he wondered how these ugly hairless creatures could survive the change. But since he could not sleep with them chattering so, he decided to see if he could think of a way to help them and get them to shut up. He decided he would go steal some fire from the sun to help the Human Beings keep warm. He found a horn and stopper. Then, that night, he hiked up the western mountain.

He saw the Sun's house was dark and that the Sun was asleep. So he sneaked in and took some coals from Sun's hearth and put them in the empty horn and hid it in the fur of his bushy tail and started back down the mountain. But he had not noticed how much time had passed. Sun woke up. He noticed the missing fire. He came raging out of the house and said, "Who took my fire?" He looked down the mountain and spied Possum running for his life. He cupped his hands around his mouth and blew a fiery blast at possum to teach him a lesson. It caused the coals in his tail to light up. The fire burned all the hair off his tail. And that is how possum got to have a hairless tail, and how the Human Beings got fire.

Although this story differs substantially from the Greek myth of Prometheus, who was punished with a horrible sentence for giving humankind fire, it nonetheless confirms that the advent of the use of fire was of great importance around the world. In fact, most cultures have many stories that refer to the origins of the common, everyday things around them, especially those things, such as fire, which have a significant impact on their daily lives.

Joseph Campbell describes how the universality of such stories are evidence of the common origins of myth. He further notes the gradual

shift in primary totemic figures as the Human Beings migrated from
one place to another. He speaks of the shift from snake to lion, to bull,
to bear—symbols of power and transformation—as people moved
from tropical to arctic environments. As with fire, only then could they
use their knowledge to move into and across the northern temperate
zone.

People did not need to hunt that much, and gathering provided most
of their dietary needs. But once they figured out that cooked meat was
safe to eat, they could begin to exploit cooler climates. As they traveled,
they noted those natural elements and events that most impacted their
survival. These were formally embedded in their languages and oral
traditions.

Language itself could well have developed out of the early hunting
economy. Proto-languages consisting of vocal tones and gestures were
fine for close contact. But hunting requires concealment from predators
and prey alike. The human vocal mechanism has been able to duplicate
animal sounds for a lot longer than it has been able to form words. It
would have been apparent to our ancestors that it was possible to attach
a meaning to an animal sound far different than that intended by the
animal of origin itself.

Connecting by association the sound of an animal with a specific
movement or direction would have provided a fertile method of imbuing
the spaces between things with meaning. Capturing these meanings in
repetitive aural combinations imposed a new order on human awareness
and gave the people a tool whereby they could pass information from one
generation to the next. The accumulation of information in the visual and
oral traditions, and its handing down from one generation to the next, has
made all the difference in the development of human beings.

When such information was finally written down, beginning only
about several thousand years ago, it became the basis for modern
civilization. It imbued a group with power, cohesion, and a shared sense
of identity. Having always shared perceptions and habits, human beings
now shared customs, traditions, taboos, and cultural identity that dif-
fered from others around them as well. Their spiritual traditions developed to account for the unseen elements and processes in the local
environment that impacted their unique lives from day to day. Their
ceremonies and customs gave them a perceived means of accessing and
influencing the powers of nature.

Language, which was a sacred being, was a means of gathering power, and of influencing the unseen. It provided a means of entering into the spiritual world or dimension of being to benefit and sustain the localized community. Words were substantial, enabled their users to make things happen, to influence change, to benefit the group as a whole, and to transfer the communal knowledge from one generation to the next.

Thus, the stories we grow up with have shaped us and defined the limits of our world, acted as a positive filtering system telling us what to exclude and how to act in relation to our surroundings and one another. They provided culture with a means of ongoing sustenance. Contained within the oral traditions are our roots, our source, our branches, our movements, and our relationships. Culture specific understandings of our migration are thus neither right nor wrong, as they are primarily informative in nature.

So it is we have populated the world, completed the great circle of life, and developed into the many hundreds of specific cultures and nations that exist today. We have each elected to sustain and maintain those traits most useful and desirable to the community, and which help to satisfy the need for an integrated identity. We are all part of this circle, but much has happened to mislead us, to cause us to consider ourselves separate and apart from one another, because we differ in various ways. And this division is killing us.

Around ten thousand years ago in the area now known as the Mid-East, the earliest agricultural civilizations emerged. They were based upon the domestication of plants and animals and the intensification of environmental use beyond the ability of the ecological system to replenish itself. Along with plants and animals, the powers of the earth, water, wind and fire were captured to increase production of food. There was a resulting rise in population leading to the development of political states necessary for the control of the distribution of goods and services. The populations began to outgrow their surroundings. Women and children became part of a man's household property; primogeniture became the accepted means of transferring material accumulations from one generation to the next. Excess male youth was put into military and police forces to control the people and expand their territory. The old ways were destroyed, and the beginnings of the modern world came into being.

So now let us look at some who speak for the indigenous worldview which says this process is killing us all.

The Way of Death

In Leslie Silko's novel, *Ceremony,* there is a passage about the power of the word that reverberates with the dictum of many belief systems: In the beginning was the Word. From it all else emerged. Words are a form of power. With them you can influence others, nature, and the powers and forces that are evident though not always apparent, which extend into our daily lives from the unseen world and affect what happens to us.

The rather extended passage below is shortened somewhat and written in paragraphs instead of verse to save space. It refers to a time before there were any white people in the world, and how, at a convocation of people with special gifts and powers, one competitor created something terrifying:

> Long time ago in the beginning there were no white people in this world there was nothing European.... The world was already complete, even without white people.... Then it happened ... witch people got together. Some came from far away across oceans across mountains. Some had slanty eyes others had black skin. They all got together for a contest ... in dark things ... they got together to fool around in caves with their animal skins.... Finally there was only one who hadn't shown off charms or powers ... no one knew where this witch came from which tribe or if it was a woman or a man.... This one just told them to listen: 'What I have is a story.' At first they all laughed but this witch said. 'Okay go ahead laugh if you want to but as I tell the story it will begin to happen. Set in motion now set in motion by our witchery to work for us. Caves across the ocean in caves of dark hills white skin people like the belly of a fish covered with hair. They grow away from the earth they grow away from the sun then they grow away from the plants and animals. They see no life when they look they see only objects. The world is a dead thing for them the trees and rivers are not alive the mountains and stones are not alive. The deer and the bear are objects they see no life. They fear they fear the world. They destroy what they fear. They fear themselves. The wind will blow them across the ocean thousands of them in giant boats swarming like larva out of a crushed ant hill. They will carry objects that can shoot death faster than the eye can see. They will kill all the things they fear all the animals the people will starve. They will poison the water they will spin the water away there will be drought the people will starve. They will fear what they find they will fear the people they will kill what they fear. Entire villages will be wiped out they will slaughter whole tribes. Corpses for us, blood for us killing killing killing. And those they do not kill will die anyway at the destruction they see at the loss at the loss of

the children the loss will destroy the rest. Stolen rivers and mountains the stolen land will eat their hearts and jerk their mouths from the Mother. The people will starve. They will bring terrible diseases the people have never known. Entire tribes will die out covered with festered sores.... Corpses for our work ... set in motion ... by our witchery ... to work for us. They will take this world from ocean to ocean they will turn on each other they will destroy each other up here in these hills they will find rocks ... with veins of green and yellow and black. They will lay the final patterns with these rocks ... and explode everything. Set in motion now ... to destroy to kill ... performing the witchery for suffering ... torment ... still-born ... deformed ... sterile ... dead.'

So the other witches said 'Okay you win; you take the prize but what you said just now—it isn't so funny it doesn't sound so good. We are doing okay without it we can get along without that kind of thing. Take it back. Call that story back.' But the witch just shook its head at the others in their stinking animal skins, furs and feathers. 'It's already turned loose. It's already coming. It can't be called back.'

This is a powerful description of the way of death. It is the way we relate to the earth and one another today. We have captured the powers of nature, the spirits of plants and animals, and no longer relate to them spiritually. We deny the numinous, sacred quality of nature, and reject the interconnectivity of all life. And it is killing us. How have we come so far along the way of death? Why is modern humanity in general, and present-day America in particular, so intent on their own destruction? What happened in the process whereby we made this transition from prehistoric cultures to modern nations?

Basically, indigenous community is based upon shared identity. This consists of a common language used to condition the individual perceptions into forms which give rise to shared communal attitudes, values, beliefs, and behavior in relation to the natural environment and human systems. Human populations developed many languages as they diffused into unpopulated areas, and their communal responses to the environment gave rise to stable cultural formations. Each group has a tribal specific cultural heritage and political legacy.

This diffusion and spread into selected ecosystems resulted in each community finding its own way to organize itself. The way in which a culture/community with a shared responsibility adapts itself to the demands of a geographical area and environment defines its shape, or form.

This process of adaptation does not apply in the case of the peoples who developed identities and worldviews based on the patriarchal and materialistic model most common among the Anglo-Europeans. These peoples adapt the environment to their internal, reified models of how it should be organized. They do this because of their continual migration from and loss of their traditional indigenous tribal lifestyle. They also, due to their settled agricultural and industrial lifestyles, tended to build up excess wealth over time. This disempowered women, destroyed the environment, and led to the need for colonization and the development of materialist values, beliefs, and attitudes—in a word, domination by conflict and war.

This domination is best described by thinking about the models of nature and man created with the spread of scientific humanism and Christian materialism. The use of reason rather than intuition, of war rather than sharing, of a human-centered world rather than a spiritually center world, have all made a major contribution to the destruction and conflicts with us today.

American Indian peoples, in contrast, are primarily animists and communalists. They can best be described through the use of a multi-dimensional approach. This approach employs tribal specific heritage in the development of a religo-philosophic organizational model. The four dimensions of this model are:

1) **Substantive**—This dimension consists of holistic beliefs, positive mysticism, spiritual symbiosis, and the numinous tradition transmitted through oral means, behavioral modeling, and communal sharing and identity. These, in turn, encompass the general enduring essential beliefs that take tribal specific forms and underlie community activity.

2) **Structural**—This dimension describes the systematic organization of cultural knowledge within the family, clan, village community, and ecosystem matrix. This dimension sees the world as sacred, that there is a transcendent order. Human identity is extended into, and an extension of, the natural environment. The network of affiliations contains the traditions, customs, taboos, and other normative standards and forms of ritual. It also describes behavior towards others, and towards nature that guides the activities of the community as it determines its direction and governs itself in a variety of ways specific to each group.

3) **Procedural**—This dimension describes activities carried out by consensus attained through council discussion in the sub-matrices of the community. This leads to agreement by and within the community matrix at large. This is an integrational social model that governs procedures and promotes synergic social policy beneficial to the community as a whole. Symbolic expressions of the social model and the environmental code of conduct are maintained in the oral forms of advice, song, chants, prophecies, oration/speeches, stories, legends, myths and other forms of comm(unications)unity. Such views see the animals, plants, and land as relations, treating all things as spiritual forms in accordance with their relationship to all other things. These views support complete recycling of resources, respect for all parts of the environment, a ceremonial economy, and status based on generosity to name but a few components.

4) **Operational/Product**—This dimension is the operational outcome of applied cultural technology. These applications include all tacit theories and implicit ideologies. These provide the internal and external supports for social units. Each unit is produced in the form of diverse cultural expressions of community within the geographical/environmental matrix overall. The above dimensions are animistic, mystical, sacred, and numinous. They produce communities vastly different in structure and scope from Anglo-European forms.

Western forms of civilization are dead, ahistoric, useless and dysfunctional. They demystify and objectify nature. They deconsecrate the communal beliefs, values, and attitudes of the group. They desacralize the spiritual politics and ceremonial economies of indigenous forms of community. This dysfunction disempowers women and children and places them in a position of subservience. It makes them part of the economic property under a male's domination and promotes the belief that man is superior to nature and has an inherent right to control it. We are forced to adopt the materialist ethic, the linear time frame, the concept of death, and the alienating individualism that separates us from nature and one another.

Indigenous organizational forms are voluntary, and their purpose is to give rise to continuing personal, cultural and environmental renewal. Such forms give rise to living, enduring, useful, dynamic, and viable systemic community networks. These networks are cyclic perceptions of common spiritual biohistory and the shared nature of communal reality. This type of thinking is at the root of hologenics.

Indigenous communities create complimentary resource goals through reciprocal cooperation. They generate a win-win transcendent mentality and perception of common legitimate vested resource interests. They promote principled methods of negotiation, collaborative problem-solving and mutual self-empowerment. Mediated wise agreements are based on mutually acceptable resource use and commonly held complementary resource goals. The social network and institutions operate through constructive tension. They tend to support enduring moral and ethical relationships, internal conflict management, and a sense of balance which optimizes and cultivates the potential for peaceful personal, cross- and intercultural contacts.

In such social systems there is no need or use for police, jails, military forces or weapons of mass destruction. The worst punishment is exclusion. But such a response to unwanted social behavior won't work in the planetary mind. We are all connected and cannot return to being separate from the modern world. Globalization is creeping into every opening in all social bodies. It's an infectious comfort, to live in the modern world.

Anglo-European cultural forms are based on antagonistic, mutual-reciprocal competition over perceived scarce resources. This takes the form of adversarial rivalry and reactive interaction. The win-lose defensive mentality that dominates all interactions and relationships results in game-playing for the purposes of attaining a relative advantage over the perceived opponent. Further, positional superiority is achieved through litigation and arbitration, resulting in lose-lose outcomes and mutually imposed impotence.

Bargaining in the West is not mediatory, but zero-sum. Bargaining is undertaken not to benefit the whole but for exclusive goal attainment that benefits individuals or factions within the hierarchically organized social structure. This structure is based on abstract concepts of codified government and law. The conflicts which arise over reciprocally incompatible and contradictory resource goals work to the disadvantage of the greater whole, the community. This results in fragmentation, stratification, inequity, and continual disturbance and disruption. The activities of the individuals and communities over conflicting resource goals, interests, and uses are forced to conform to the cultural mainstream of a given specific tribal, social, or national group. Comfort is used to control the public.

The way of life of the indigenous peoples and the way of death of the Anglo-European peoples are so in contrast as to be incompatible. They are mutually exclusive, and diametrically opposed to one another. The way of the materialists has overshadowed the way of the animists, and the current state of our world reflects their antagonism.

Those who moved from prehistory through agriculture to industry, and towards an information base for their civilizations, have suffered greatly. The oppositional views, distorted perceptions, twisted values, fallacious beliefs, and conflict-ridden attitudes which dominate the world today are all a result of the widening gulf between the natural peoples and the mechanical peoples. Their languages and societies must be ultimately recombined. Reconstruction of exclusive worldviews will do much to prevent a cancerous, virulent, pathogenic global state, based on greed and the manipulation of want for the purpose of profit, to continue to fester and grow. We must turn to the world beyond this one, to the spiritual union of natural culture and industrial politics if we are to prevent further dehumanization.

The World of Tomorrow

What will the world become when we have achieved our global union? How will we live? The uses of the environment will become more oriented towards the common good rather than profit. The boundaries between nation-states, religions, and the diverse ethnic communities that we see today will gradually dissolve.

As the global telecommunications network is completed, most people will be able to instantly access anyone they choose anywhere on the globe. All that's needed is the tenth generation of computing devices. The impoverished masses of the developing world will rise up against those who seek to dominate them for profit. They will rebel, as the rich get richer, as the greed and profit at the expense of, and by the exploitation of, others continues to spread. The resources we share will be exhausted, energy supplies used up, environments ravaged and peoples destroyed. When the dust of global conflict settles, we'll see a more equalized flow of goods and services through the lifelines of the world. Economic imbalances will be rectified, and the resistance between our parts, east and west will diminish.

A more focused worldview will emerge. It will be integrative and holistic in nature. It will unify more than it divides; it can be universally embraced without any compromise or loss of localized identity, tradition, or beliefs. Centralized governmental functions will be more evenly distributed among concerned localities, and the interconnected human world will take over its affairs with vigor and hope. That we have begun this change is a fact already. But it is not recognized or accepted by those with a vested interest in the maintenance of inequality,

Corporations and their governmental minions destroy the world. They follow the way of death to line their coffers. They exploit the work force for their own benefit, which prevents the development and production of beneficent, benign technology, such as using hydrogen fuel. They are promoted by the continuance of inequitable economic systems. They will be brought down, gradually, and the system will be given back to the human beings to use for the greater good and the benefit of all.

The oil cartels and the weapons makers, the telecommunications giants and usurers of the banking systems—all will be brought low in time, be it in ten, a hundred, or a thousand years. We who are the Human Beings know this. We see that time is not a factor in these events coming to pass, and are certain in our knowledge that the way of the circle of life must and will be sustained and embraced by all those who wish to live rather than go extinct. Those among us charged with keeping these ancient and timeless understandings alive have been doing so for forty thousand years, despite what the modern, materialist peoples think or believe. We have done so as fully conscious, responsible, human beings even until today, and will continue to do so into the next century and beyond, until peace returns.

The Way of the 21st-Century Shaman

The modern shaman is a transcendent being. Such a one uses every available means to create hologenic knowledge and liberate human beings from illusion, doubt, fear, suffering, and pain. The rituals and ceremonies of all peoples of every place and time are available to draw upon, and new ways can be created from the old.

As in the times past, the shaman seeks to cure the ills of the people, to return the community to balance. Through the natural allies in the realms of minerals, plants, animals, the human beings seek out and find those elements of our system which are distorted, bent, twisted or warped. They reveal elements inconsistent with the harmonious function of the individual, the community, and the system as a whole within which we all exist.

Even today there are those who are devoted to aiding the disturbed in their struggle toward wholeness. Likewise, these persons aid the well developed and matured towards transcendence and liberation from illusion.

They guide others in the ways of true freedom: freedom from fear, want and lack of means to fulfill basic needs. Further, they help those struggling in the throes of addiction. Becoming dependent on that which destroys is fueled by ignorance of, or failure to reach, inherent potentials. This ignorance is fostered by those in power to maintain control over the working peoples.

Those who comfort others are the spiritual beings. Their patterns of being were written in the book of life before the beginning. They are primary functionaries in the original singularity. Their purpose is to achieve full mutuality during the return to unity. In this unity the individual self returns to the universal Self. The localized mind enters global planetary awareness. The human sphere is returned to balance.

Joseph Campbell speaks of those who create myth rather than interpret or merely live by it. These are the truly creative peoples. Now they will be the source of the emerging planetary mythos. This reconstructed worldview must evolve as did the ancient ways of the natural peoples and the recently developed ways of the modern materialist peoples—in response to the new environment we've created. If successful, the adoption of this revised view will result in the dissolution of political and corporate boundaries and limits. It will bring an end to the evil, the greed and the profit motive that stifles creativity. We will see the emergence of a planetary order wherein all are joined yet autonomous. Personal responsibility, familial understanding, community partnership, group cooperation, and ecological conservatism and preservation will sustain our mutual interests. These will provide the foundation for a reorganized, global human intelligence.

There are no hard and fast rules. The shaman makes the rules. The shaman can be of either gender, any age, of various species even, but for certain can emerge within any culture, time, or place. The shaman existed before the world began, before the universe came into being, and is without beginning or end. The shaman's most powerful tool is the word that is an expression of the power of creation, the universal mind, the energy in formation of life itself. To the shaman the universe is less like a machine, and more like a great idea.

The shaman lives in many worlds, realms, and domains simultaneously; forever awake, forever conscious. Such a being exists as a luminous sphere whose illumination comes from within the core of creation. To the shaman everything is transparent and clear; everything begins and ends in light. Time ceases to have any meaning when everything is both possible and complete. The path he or she takes returns forever to the beginning.

The power of creation contains, and is contained by, all. The shaman is the bearer of the power of creation, the medium through which it flows into the world, and the means by which the people are made whole, able to express nature's own genius, part of the great circle of life, and set free from the bondage of limited identification with the ephemeral and temporal things and states of this world.

The shaman is joined with nature, in every place and time able to communicate with and utilize the powers of all the plants and animals and elemental beings. The shaman knows the old prayers and ceremonies and rituals, but renews them according to the needs of the time and place. We are all joined with the shaman and are led, each in our own way, to the center of creative and regenerative understanding. We are led to the heart of love, and beyond this physical realm into the infinite.

Unique and original forms of organization will emerge over the next couple of centuries as we adapt to the continually changing conditions we are creating. We will use up the oil and find new sources of power to maintain a minimal energy environment that sustains and does not destroy. We will be free of the abstract economy of currency and all will receive what they need and give what they can. The military technology will be disassembled and rebuilt as implements that will help us increase our declining ability to produce enough food for all.

The women of the earth will again rise to prominence when they take control of the reproductive life of the world as they adjust the birth rate. The number of allowable children born year to year will be dependent upon the available environmental resources. No more deficit spending! We will operate within our limits and improve our efficiency. Women will regain their rights as equals. Need will be the basis for determining what one does or does not possess.

Conflicts between identity groups will lessen as we overcome the artifice of national, racial, and religious boundaries. This will allow spiritual politics to assert itself as the dominant form of regulation. A government of, by, and for all people will arise. It will fulfill the original democratic ideals of cultures based on leading by following, by putting others first, by getting out of the way of free trade, and ending dominance and aggression which destroys. We will take care of all our relations in the natural world we inhabit, which gives us our bodies and the opportunity to experience self-awareness in order that the power of creation can find and relate to and identify with itself. The world of nature and the world of culture will be the same.

This is no utopian vision, no idealized state, no imaginary projection. This is what we must and will do for the benefit of the coming generations. It may take the destruction of many peoples and much of some environments. It may demand the end of much that was cherished when we were separated from our original unity. But so be it. Be prepared, be strong, be ready for change. Otherwise you will perish. Look to the shaman among you, seek them out and partake of their wisdom, as they are the lovers and teachers within us all.

The way of the 21st-century shaman is the same as it has always been. But times have changed. We have gone from the multiple to the binary, from the analog to the digital. We have begun to move away from the divisive towards the unifying, from the broken hoop to the restored circle. We are headed from the localized identity to the global, from the bounded state to the planetary mind, from the spatio-temporal to the universal. We have explored and found, destroyed and created, lived and died for millions of generations. We will continue if we will it so, if we create within our communities and ourselves the clear pathways into a glorious future.

This is what One Wolf taught me, what my elders and ancestors and all my relations have given so that all might live together in the great circle of life on earth. It is up to us, no matter our path, our history, our heritage, our worldview. We have been lost for a long time. Now we are found. We are the Human Beings, the First People.

VII

Beyond This World

Integrative Systemic Response

EACH NERVE PLEXUS HAS PARTICULAR RESPONSES to the integration of biological, emotional, and psychological systems. For instance, when the lower nerve plexus—that associated with the most basic of physical intake and elimination—is integrated, one feels a great sense of relief and satisfaction and rightness when foods and waste products are smoothly and easily obtained, eaten, and processed into various useful products. These are the resultants of activity in day-to-day life—the vector space of our being and experience.

Likewise, when the procreative and reproductive systems reach a state of integration, one moves beyond the mere self-indulgence of pleasure and orgasm. One is enabled with appropriate practice to move beyond into the domains of ecstasy and bliss. Such states are described and depicted by the ancients in their complex instructional manuals and discourses on the super-physical benefits of sexual activity.

When the male attains full control over erection and orgasm, he transcends the sexual drives and is able to have sexual intercourse as often as desired. He is able to control the orgasm, so that his energies are not depleted, by various degrees of controlled release. He can see the falling away of mere lust as the energies then rise into the higher and more complex systems of the body.

When a woman gains complete control over her sensuality and recreative power, she likewise is able to leave behind her fears, inhibitions, repressed memories and withheld feelings. She can then find in herself a sense of safety, strength, and security that is not derived from outer things. It is derived instead from unifying her female power with that which occurs in all of nature, and of which she is part and expression.

The fullness of the maturation of the nervous system is an ongoing process, not a goal or event outcome. As maturation is achieved at one level, higher level possibilities are revealed. The sense of identity can be expanded beyond the individual self, into others, all of nature, all sentient life, and finally to pure being itself. At this point identity expands into the actualized Self that is whole and complete and able to be at rest while remaining fully aware and involved in the commonplace.

The third system is centered in the organs that are involved in transformation of material substances into usable materials and energies. Those organic sub-systems are centered in the general area of the solar plexus—stomach, liver, spleen, bladders, kidneys and the like. When the third system is integrated, it incorporates the natural intake and output functions of the first and second systems, the powerful regenerative drives of food consumption and reproduction.

These three then join and move into the central power system and are then all expressed in the ability to simply think. One can then bring thoughts to life and material form. It becomes possible to manifest dreams, intuitions, thoughts, and engage in actions that have as their natural outcome a harmonic and dynamic balance. Equilibrium in relating to the material world results from material and physical well-being. These three systems connect us to others and the world.

The fourth system is that which directs the flows of fluids and gases physically. It governs the flow of endocrine and lymphatic systems, and the nervous power. Stored power in the nervous system is then released from bondage to non-integrated lower functions and their dependence on instinct and other lower brain stem and mid-brain functions. It then expands from the center upward and outward. The result is that compassion and love for all sentient beings becomes the primary directive for operational activity. Within the brain, then, the raw biological energy moves in a harmonic fashion through the limbic system, bringing a calm, rested, peaceful demeanor and relaxed feeling in all situations.

The nervous energy is then liberated into the outer layers of the neocortex. The internal feedback systems allow the nerve plexus centered in the throat, thyroid, vocal cords, and linguistic associative areas to shape all linguistic outputs. Speech and writing become expressive of that which unifies and heals, brings comfort and ends distress. Speech uses raw sound and other more complex vibratory phenomenon (hymns, chants, liturgy, poetry, incantation, invocation, evocation, provocation, etc.) that take one beyond self. This music carries one into the greater unified sense of being human and living fully. Universal mindedness is then able to overcome divisions and boundaries and convey to others the experience of wholeness and functional systemic integration. The fifth system then takes us beyond this world.

Once the power of creation has been purified and the systems trained to carry the clarified energies, then the sixth system, including pituitary and frontal lobe areas that have to do with neural and psychological function, is further activated. This activation increases one's sense of that which is not only within the frequency ranges of the physical sensory systems alone, but beyond. One can begin to perceive that which is bordering on the edges of being obvious but not visible, evident but not substantial, clearly existing yet intangible. Proper discipline and instruction in the sciences and arts of sound/vibration can be gleaned from poetry, music, neurolinguistics and psycho-acoustics. One becomes able to read voices and sound with a multi-band awareness. One senses a multi-modal, multiplex perceptual process that reveals many channels of information. One becomes able to use various forms of language and communication to directly stimulate the various nervous system channels, organic systems, and cerebral activity and areas. When this happens, one can actually calm, heal, and stimulate integrated awareness in other receptive individuals and groups. One develops hypnotic language that is irresistible and can effect changes in perception.

When fully integrated, the nervous system is able to grow as a whole and mature into harmonic function. Then the self is no longer bound to the drives governing food, sex, money, power over others, control, profit and competition. The higher cortex can begin to function in a state of hyperconsciousness within which all becomes clear, transparent, fully what it is. We can then see patterns of light and energy and space rippling in the currents, tides, and eddies of gravitational force. It becomes evident that pure energy is organized into what our limited sensory array perceives as the material and natural world in which we live and function.

In this state deep in the seventh system, one is able to willingly enter into the void, empty spaces of the universe and draw therefrom the power of creation itself. One can channel it into the nervous system in such a way as to convey through the individual a vision of being that is complete. This "visionary humanism" is no longer fragmented, divided, a broken circle full of alienation and separateness. It becomes an integrated systemic response to being human, unified, whole, and on the edge of the state of singularity. Only a few fortunate ones achieve the unbounded state, which transcends borders, definitions, limits and time. This state of being leads us to a reunion with the power of creation from which all our awareness flows, and in which we, the first people, the human beings, have been joined since the dawn of our awareness some forty thousand years ago.

The current political and social states exist for the purpose of power and profit. Those who identify with these states enforce separateness and keep others unaware of our unity and our power as a species. They are thus by choice perpetually irresponsible, and hence immature. They work for the benefit of those who promote the illusions that keep the few in comfort and wealth while the majority suffers. The majority searches for those basic elements that make it possible for them to rise above the lower systems of the hierarchy of needs for air, water, food, warmth, and interaction with place and people. They desire in the soul to rejoin all our relations.

When such baser requirements are satisfied, we are then able to join together into a mass singularity, a singular body of aware beings working for the benefit and good of all people, nature and life. We agree with those who have mastered their systems and achieved functional maturity. They show us the way to establish an immortal identity and awareness though whatsoever integrative tradition or practice they have engaged in.

This is then the function and purpose of human beings: to grow, mature, and share awareness. Through this, all life prospers and grows together. We gradually and ever more fulfill and realize our nature and full potentials. Such a clear vision of this is only accessed through many years of practice and study. We who are of the esoteric orders are no more or less than others. We are perhaps more fortunate in terms of our gifts, but as a result we bear a deep love and an even greater sense of responsibility for being of benefit and service to other. Mature beings are pretty much the same everywhere and cannot argue or disagree, for they have seen the singular, know that One which all the differentiated forms and beings both contain and are contained by. This is the nature of the integrated soul.

As such, we who are chosen for this task are working in a deep reality, in the fields of quantum flux and pure gravitation. Our lives are dedicated to the proposition that all peoples are singular in their core identities. We are joined, in constant contact with, and able to be aware of one another in ways that seem to violate the laws of physics. However, that has always been the case with those who work directly with gravity and quantum theory.

Our genetic codes are composed of a sort of music made of four proteins and enzymes. The physical patterns and their codes, which govern our physical beings, are immortal, global, unitary, and singular. We are all related, and there is only one world with many peoples. We must get along and benefit one another, like it or not. We are both aware of this and willing to embark on the adventure of maturation, or we refuse to acknowledge or accept it and remain forever sheep and the children of sheep.

We are radiant beings. All else comes of that. So it has been remembered, in oral traditions, in the dreams of seers, the songs of the bards, the texts of the ancient esoteric orders, and the teachers who recite them. We also know this truth from the poems of the word ringers, the equations of quantum physics, the genetic code, and the collective memory conscious and unconscious. This awareness is always with us and available to any who wish to enter into the fullness of true mature adulthood and integrated systemic response.

Who Are We?

As in the development of the fetal brain described earlier, basic life energies combine in the gamete. The code is set, the proteins manufactured, cells grow in undifferentiated profusion and only gradually, after many days, start to take on the unique properties that distinguish one type from another. All do as they must, and no one usually knows what the greater purpose or function of their work is. Gradually, as they work together, a body is formed with trillions of parts and interconnections, which will grow and develop its own identity. The body is fused from the basic elements of quantum, subatomic, atomic, molecular, chemical, cell, organismic, and superorganismic elements that give rise to the physical, emotional, mental and spiritual traits one has. From the combination of many such bodies, the shapes of societies and other identity groups are formed.

When the systemic elements begin to create the bodily parts, they make an ear here, and eye there, a toe, a nose. In great profusion the cranial cells begin to form the fetal brain. This complex, multi-layered system, with its many areas of sensory, perceptual, cognitive and other functions, gives rise to what will, if viable, become one of us, a human being. Each human being will extend his or her identity by exploring all the boundaries, definitions, and nature of self, language, other, and environment.

This is no different from what we humans do on the global scale. Have we not given the planet eyes to see to the edges of creation? Have we not given a voice to light, radio waves and other electromagnetic spectra? Do we not as well lend the earth our ears, to hear the cooling hiss of microwaves from the general background radiation, with a global network of dish antennae and computers?

We are the ones who are creating across the earth the basic elements and components of a global identity. We provide those aspects of life that, when combined in us and joined in our interactions with ourselves, others, and the environment, result in an infinite net of expanding identity that will comprise the global mind. Those who are ready and able to endure the dropping away of their old frames of reference, the melting away of the old identity and development of a new sense of who we are, will feel their own identity riding the waves of energy outward into infinity.

We are mounds of earth, electric walking mud puddles stumbling around on calcium stilts. We are the ocean's way of exploring dry places. The human beings are the first people, all joined together, like it or not! Like Robert Frost said, "People work together whether they work together or apart." He also noted it is human nature to be "neither out far nor in deep." We are making a world awaken, making mirrors within and without. We are mirrors reflecting into the depths of sea and sky. When all our reflective capacity is put together, we see within ourselves the truth. There will come a time when we are joined in this essential awareness, when the primal unity of the biosphere overwhelms the divisions of the social, political, and economic world. However, there will never be a time without conflicts, organizational structures, or those woes and miseries that attend our short tours in this life.

There will be a time when we will all become truly educated and takes full responsibility for our lives and the results of our actions. Basic needs will be provided for. We all will become ever more free of the need for paternalistic governments and exploitative economies. Such organizational forms all contribute to and engage in pointless ethnic, religious, and national conflicts for power and profit. The basic greed and lust, which have been conditioned into us in many cultures, societies, and civilizations, can be redirected into beneficial, non-violent courses and channels. We are here to realize our potentials, perform our function of unifying the planetary mind, and then surrender ourselves back to the source from which we emerge and return. There is nothing new or remarkable about that. But the information that is so ancient has simply not been expressed coherently and completely in modern English.

The words we use to communicate are what make so much of our world possible. Words are the glue of culture, as love is the glue of family and community, as gravity is the glue of the cosmos. We are to find the most effective and useful ways to connect across our differences in friendly fashion. Tolerate ambiguity. That is the demand of the time. Look beyond the limits of self and seek to realize the potential for full humanity.

We use words to define, and they use us to travel. Each phone, phoneme, syllable, word and sentence, when joined with others, creates the world and gives it meaning. Words are the means by which we organize the many forms of energy and matter competing for our attention, seeking our comfort, and providing our experience.

The Living Word gives us the power to relate across time and distance, to join in understanding, and share in who we are. Each and every word, depending on its elements, has its own specific gravity. The energy of the system expressed in the word attracts and repels. The greater the extent of the meaning of a sound, the more of these attractive or repellent qualities and quanta the word or thought has.

I believe it possible to formulate equations (though I am not the one to do so) that quantify the nature of language and meaning. I have, however, worked on a conceptual approach to this for years. How are we to define that which has no measurable mass, is insubstantial yet evident, obvious yet not apparent, real but without form? As such, the nature of language and meaning pose special and yet unresolved questions. Perhaps this question is best answerable in the domains of systems theory, quantum dynamics and neurolinguistics: Hologenics.

And to finally define, to more completely answer this problem, is to come to a greater understanding of who we are. We can come to understand ever more deeply how we are connected. We will know what we must do in order to live and speak well. We are the first people, and human beings, and must be free, informed, and able to make wise decisions in the best interests of all concerned, and thus become ever more fully human.

Quantum Recreation

We are joined in an unrecognized and unrealized singularity, we human beings. The coherent codes of immortal genes pass from body to body undisturbed. These codes govern the creation of physical bodies from which the pure precipitate of imagination falls in an unending rain of cells, bodies, houses, societies and worlds unknown and undreamed of. On the quantum level, we are all connected. Research in a Swiss particle accelerator proved that either of two photons that have been in contact and diverge will simultaneously experience whatever the other does instantaneously! So are we humans joined, no matter how far apart or for how long. At the speed of light there is not two.

We have dreams and do all we can to imagine ourselves. We define the world, account for the unseen, are born and die at the rate of hundreds per second. We are the human beings, the singular race, the first people. We can reflect, know that we know that we know we know. So we know that there is a Knower immortal, infinite, undefined, and apart from us, yet within us at the same time. This is the basic dichotomy with which we each must deal.

As such this is the root of our biospiritual unity. We are joined at the quantum level. We are forever recreating self, other, world and cosmos by reconfiguring the designs and patterns inherent in our makeup. Change the way we use words and we alter our perceptions. Alter perception and we alter thereby the objects of perception. Alter the objects and change reality.

When we focus on this, we enter a chaotic flux where limited individual self dissolves into greater human Self. When this occurs and is not effectively dealt with, there is often a breakdown of the ego integrity. Sometime the psyche fails. Even pathology and other aberrations occur on occasion. But if we do not fully experience and completely deal with this process of transformation, then we are forever lost, alienated, fragmented, incoherent, and constantly seeking gratification, rest and peace, but unable find it.

We must die to the molecular to enter the quantum singularity at the heart of all being. We must embrace the chaos in order to find the peace. We must surrender our life to the greater whole in order to be reborn into the immortal One. This is the nature of quantum recreation. This is the source of true sanity and peaceful existence, of our unity and meaning in life.

Ionic UFOs

Charles Fort, the collector of anomalies and oddities, said, "We're living at the bottom of somebody's pond, and it ain't ours." Carl Jung thought that UFOs were projections of the collective unconscious. After broad and detailed research and review of reports over the last one thousand years in his work, *Flying Saucers,* Jung eliminated for the most part the possibility that aliens are visiting earth. He also rejected the notion the phenomena can be fully explained as geomagnetic or human created atmospheric events.

Watching documentaries on deep-sea exploration, one can peer into the most marvelous depths at creatures that make their own lights. Such creatures live on molecular compounds gushing hot and sulfurous from the heart of the world. We are still attempting to classify and understand them. How can they live under the pressures so far down in a world without visible light?

It took generations for Americans to learn shipbuilding, metalwork, etc., and build the first ironclad and submersible naval vessels. Thousands of man-hours are required to dig up the ores and smelt the metals, form the sphere and outfit the bathysphere or submarine, which is capable of entering the dark depths. We shatter the silence and flash bright lights in peculiar patterns. We blind and deafen the creatures below, and occasionally reach out to grab and abduct the denizens of the deep for study in our world miles above.

We can generate patterns of activity in the brain, externalize and manifest our thoughts. This is the meaning of magic and results in the diversity and plethora of technological and manufactured items and media in which we create the world wherein we exist. We have created a shell of sorts, our material civilization. It is like a giant scabbing disease, an artificial layer on the surface of the globe. We live within the shell, out of touch with earth and sky. We collect our resources and burn them in ceaseless fire.

Strip away the outer layers of a city, and all that's left are the electrons magically zinging along the molecular grids we have made to carry them as packets and bundles of power. Our ability to drop down to the bottom of the sea is one product of our magic. Another is our manufacturing of a vast and fine literature and science. These beautiful explanations and equations exist side-by-side, along with such lame and uncreative productions as our explanations for UFOs.

UFO events are known, and best described, by a set of characteristics familiar to most of us. Their shapes and speeds, flight patterns and phenomenology are all described. They are said to cause fluctuations or shutdowns in the power grid, bright flashing lights, strange hums, buzzes and other sounds. There is even a developing mythos of abductees. It seems these spheres from above occasionally reach out and abduct denizens from the pond at the bottom of which we live, the vast soup of atmosphere, down here in the cracks and crevices of the deep.

A friend of mine says fire is the physical expression of the eating habits of a fourth-dimensional being which likes to feed on cellulose. I think there must be infinitely many dimensions and universes, and what we see is but a pale shadow of what exists. We are subject to the narrow ranges and limitations of our sensory abilities. Just imagine how nonexistent humans are to ants, or to microbes deep in the soil. We are known only by our effects, as we are so vast, huge, and insensible that we cannot be perceived or defined in their terms.

In our upper atmosphere there exist various ionized gases. If they are gathered and compressed into a sphere or disc, they would likely, under the extreme pressures of the deep gaseous atmospheric ocean where the solid elements begin, give off patterns of light, make peculiar noises, and seem to be able to take off and move with unbelievable speed in any direction. The inhabitants of the domains and dimensions of the upper atmosphere would also be prone to occasionally taking one of we human beings home to the sky for further study. Meanwhile those of us left below must somehow try to find a way to define, rationalize, or explain away what appears to be happening. We're living at the bottom of somebody's pond, and it definitely ain't ours.

All the characteristics of what we loosely refer to as UFOs are easily explained—they come from the ionized elements of the planetary mind!

Building a "Flying Saucer"

When I was in college, I was walking through an alternative bookstore when a little book almost leaped off the shelf and into my hand. It was an odd little book. It was a written rendition of the oral recitation containing the essence of an ancient belief system originating in Japan before the Buddha came. It was called "ko-shinto"—meaning old Shinto.

It took me fifteen years of rereading repeatedly to understand what it was getting at. Human beings build their world and society and culture by organizing the vibrations of sounds that literally create the world! What an idea! Modern research does indicate that words shape and define perception and actions based thereon. This is interesting stuff, very abstract and philosophical, archaic and difficult.

In this book, of most interest, was a section at least fifteen hundred years old, that defined how to build a "flying saucer"! "Absurd," I thought. But over time and study I came to understand that the general idea was to create and use a "craft"—i.e. the technical skills attendant the arranging of sound—that would result in a vehicle that would allow one to explore the universe! We create our world by making words to name it. That is why the symbols developed later to represent the sounds were each considered sacred.

As such, the planetary mind, named and defined herein, is another step, in a centuries long process of continually adapting to and redefining our collective human experience. By making the sounds, by defining the process and nature of creation, we seed our awareness with sacred beings, gods if you will, that will guide humanity into a global awareness of the planetary mind.

Like the Navajo say, it is through human beings that the gods are given voice, and through that voice they sing the world into being each day in their recitations. All things are sacred in such a universe. All of creation is ours. We are responsible for maintaining our universe and its description. In this way we are sacred beings as well. This being so, we must perfect our craft if we wish to soar through the sky on the wings of eagles.

Using such a "craft" does indeed allow one to travel to, move within, and go beyond this world into other dimensions of feeling, thought, and understanding. We must, of course, be free of worldly attachments and entanglements in order to achieve lift-off into the cosmos, but we can do it.

We just have to let go and give enough of ourselves to the craft of creation.

The "Tachyon Body"

There is a shadow of the physical body, which corresponds to the cellular carbon-based photon-based body. The difference is that this shadow is traveling faster than light! To be able to focus our songs like angels, or spirit beings or gods, is to become aware of the universe as a contracting entity. In order to travel vast distances at light speed, one must be perfectly still so that everything eventually goes by and we go backward in time. Instead of our moving forward, we must wait for time to go by us.

We see evidence of this shadow in the microwave background radiation. When we look through our incredible lenses across the sky, back to the beginning, we are seeing the results of something that has already happened long ago, upwards of fifteen billion years so far. I refer to the actual event that preceded our universe in space and time as a body made of particles that move faster than light. Sort of. The impossible velocity is achieved not by moving, but by remaining still enough to feel the precession back before the beginning. The Bible notes that we can be still and know God. In stillness we can feel this.

The tachyon body leaves a trail of free quarks connecting it to its mates in the photon body. Like the way our shadow is connected to our body, but not exactly. The energy in formation can be translated between domains through the genetic code. The genetic code is our life record, the enzymatic music of the soul, patterns of amino acid production and solar conversion sequences. This would provide some basis for the idea of synchronicity and the notion of telepathy. It might provide a basis for finding out why current research indicates that any two photons which have been in contact at any given space-time coordinate, will, after diverging, react simultaneously when one or the other experiences a change of state.

Like twins, what one experiences, no matter the distance or time, the other photon knows at the same time. This apparently violates the physical laws. But we are dealing here with metaphysics, or a level of physics not yet penetrated by our observations. At any rate, when my genetically active and derived form of current consciousness identifies with the tachyon body, my material life appears to have already happened. It seems to be behind me, resulting in a strange sort of deja vu as I, apparently and essentially, rewrite what I did long ago, in my actual universe.

Hallucinogenic and psychotropic products are suppressed and regulated by society because they represent a means of overcoming the unconscious induction of boundaries of self, other and society. In other words, the hallucinogenic, dream state is actually our normal form of tachyonic awareness. Thus, society is a mass shared hallucination. Natural awareness, unbounded, undifferentiated is our primary type of consciousness. So, society as a whole can't allow citizens to see into, or experience the truth of our shared global and universal reality. Our nature as photonic and tachyonic beings is subsumed under organismic and material shells—our spacesuit—and we are lost.

Once one begins to accelerate to the photon barrier through the perfection of meditation and is able to see, understand, and relate to their immortal form of being, one realizes that one is free. The trust sets one free. One is vibrating so much faster than the space suit that the phase lock breaks down. We then see the temporal nature of all material and cellular existence, which then frees us to realize that we cannot be attached to anything, as all is in flux and ever changing. This does not allow for easy control of populations.

So, America outlawed and refused to find a proper use for mind-altering plants. They have refused as well to allow the development of ritual passages into adulthood that are ultimately freeing. Free people, true human beings, know they live in an unbounded state and are in complete control of what they do. The governments and corporations that control populations for the sake of power and profit will only subsidize substances that increase productivity and baffle the brain. That is why horribly addictive plants like coffee and tobacco are universal, while marijuana, mushrooms and cacti that alter consciousness and reveal the truth of the human beings are not.

Contemplating one's immortality armors the soul, so to speak, so that no material or other form of attachment can occur. Attachments induce drag and slow the tachyonic body down due to the accretion in the brain. One becomes snagged in the illusion and starts thinking the photonic and material domains are all that is.

Yet the darkness we see is but the limit of our own senses. All that we cannot see is what truly is. So, to get beyond the limits of sensory reality one must shed the earthly shell. This allows the energy in formation underlying identity to diffuse, disperse, return or make the transition from photonic reality into the tachyonic domain. Once one has made the transition—whether alive and earth-bound or after the physical life has expired—the universe is turned inside out. It reverses itself, and forever returns to the beginning, the source. Whether expanding or contracting, the whole is an integrated system. Its appearance is dictated by the nature and perceptual means and capacity of the observer.

In the tachyonic state there is no time or space, as we know it in our universe. We exist everywhere at the same time, and can focus our awareness on/to any point without losing our freedom and becoming slave to the appearance of spatial-temporal limitation. The limits, definitions, and boundaries that contain and comfort those who are still immature bring them comfort. They identify with limited worldviews to which they feel they must cling for their salvation. These limits are useful in the bounded state of chrysalis, as they help us orient ourselves during the transformation. We need directions, especially if we come together in this stormy place and time.

Such explains the popularity of political figures, demagogues, dictators, and those who seek to capitalize on the chaos of the times. The immature will turn to anyone who appears to be a central force to gather around. As Yeats said, "the center cannot hold." We are spiraling down ever further into the mud. As earthlings, it is up to us to learn about why and how we are imprisoned on this world. We are deaf, dumb, and blind in sensory terms, ever forgetful of our photonic origins. We must face the difficult task of seeing beyond if we are to glimpse ourselves in our immortal tachyonic form.

Once free again, we are able to work without any attraction to the undeveloped and immature of the earth. We step out of our space suits, return to the stars and beyond to the beginning. We are alpha and omega in the state of singularity, which is the nexus of harmony and dissonance, appearing as a voracious black hole when it is actually the door between universes.

Moral Values, Super Ego, Social Norms

The family provides firm grounding in models and examples of conflict resolution. Without an application of the understandings gained in the primary unit of conditioning, neither individual nor society will function effectively. Neither can mature in accord with each system's developmental potential.

As in the fetus, where general systems differentiate into the discrete, diverse, and various parts of the anatomical and physiological body, so as well does the person and the society. As a person experiences and learns more, picking up speed and forming new connections between neurons, self and others, and events, so do societies interact across vast distances instantly. They become more diverse, for the unstoppable process of globalization and greater connectivity will only increase in the coming decades.

When children experience environments with too little structure, where their freedom is greater than their ability to cope, they have no idea of the results of their actions. They do not consider others; they are not able to assess the potential and real impact of their interactions with others in any but the most rudimentary way. Familial and societal dysfunctions are based in this conflict between the need for both freedom and order.

Without a common sense regarding the most effective mannerisms and ways to communicate with minimal conflict, misunderstanding and disorder will reign. Social norms must be understood, whether followed or not. The moral values of a culture or subculture, the ways of thought and life, and the things they are wrapped up in are assimilated into the young by osmosis. They learn by absorption and conditioning how to most effectively fulfill their wants and needs for the basics of life. Beyond that, they mimic these structures in their play, developing attention and fostering emotional growth. When one's sense, or the sense of one's group, is lacking—as when one does not understand what amounts to the collective way, the superego, the external structures within which we exist—communication is distorted, conflict arises, and overall effectiveness and efficiency diminish.

Moral values are not unchanging. But they are consistent over time when shared by a group in agreement about their makeup and nature. Moral, as well as ethical, behavior is to a great degree based upon and reinforced by the absorbed mythos, the belief system one has learned. In America there is a wide variety of operational mythoi. Each is no more relevant than any other to the dominant vision institutionalized in our political and economic systems and shared by all in the mainstream of society. The dominant view in our day is based upon science, industry, and technology, and at odds with the ancient and universal bio-spiritual understanding shared by all prehistoric peoples. That view, first contained in oral traditions, was made manifest in common language, the spiritual traditions, and ways of life realized locally with great diversity. It is difficult to come to agreeable terms in the home, the family, and our society regarding how to deal with the moral breakdown that is progressing straight out of our differences.

A person needs a firm sense of what's allowed, what's taboo, what's polite and what's rude. They need to know the proper mannerisms, speech patterns, values and mores common among their own, and other identity groups of their locality. They need to know this in order to exist and interact effectively, mate, reproduce, and engage in commerce and cultural activities. It does not matter what the basis is for one's beliefs about what to do and how to live. What is important is that each of us has such beliefs, and is willing and able to share them with other people. As long as one has some model to emulate, one can learn what's needed.

Freud would have loved modern America. It's a living laboratory, a writhing poem across the nightmare-infested landscape of the ancients, and a gathering of most every physical and psychological type. We are forming a body that will eventually be so joined in coherent activity that all previous definitions and forms of identity will gradually fade away. The old rigid, limited definitions of self will break apart as surely as the dark cloud of unknowing from which the truth walks naked and without shame. It is up to each of us to develop our own strong identity, sense of morality, values, ethics, and mores.

We must educate ourselves to be more than blind followers of archaic codes. We cannot allow ourselves to be like the legions of lost ancestors who died under the sword of monarchy and papacy, in tyranny and moral anarchy. We must always join together to transcend our individual limitations, as persons, companies, and nation-states. Yet we must also never lose sight of our own unique and beautiful familial and cultural identity. We must find, and provide for others, models for resolution of conflict based on fact, reason, and shared understanding of our underlying biosocial unity regardless of our differences.

This education begins and ends in the family unit. It is in the values which sustain it that our true strength lies, and what must be taught to each and every child. Values will lower crime, divorce, violence and other virulent pathogenic forms of thought and behavior and result in a better world for all peoples. The only wars are in each one of us, and within is where the solution will be found.

The End of Terror

Terrorists use fear to manipulate the subjects of their horrifying acts. Only the fearless know the end of terror. All religions are equal in their share of truth. But our sensory array is so narrowly limited in terms of perceptual bandwidth that we are pretty much deaf, dumb, and blind when it comes to seeing and understanding what's really going on in our world, our universe, and ourselves.

All legitimate states are equal under universally agreed upon tenets of constitutional law. In nature we are by no means equal, but under the laws we agree to accept that, in order to receive the benefits of our society and world, we all have equal value. Still, there's a lot to be said for being able to buy the best justice possible. But this results in inequitable dispensing of the law.

All people are, each of us, a sovereign and subject of our own and society's choices. Our decisions and agreements as to policy and procedures must be shared and uncorrupted by that which cannot be given to all the same. Thus the founders of America agreed to remove all metaphysical reference from our social agreement, the Constitution of the United States. Too many kings and popes and others had been prone to using metaphysics as a justification for abuse.

John Locke wrote about his vision of social contract theory nearly five hundred years ago and removed reliance on deity for authority (what was called the "divine right of kings"). Instead, each of us was granted sovereignty when we moved to a land viewed as open and endless. We fought and died to gain the right to make our own decisions as a group by agreement of a plurality of eligible members of society: the voter and the electorate. We have the right to choose how we will live as human beings.

There is only one human race, one world we share, and one state within which we live our lives. There are, of course, real differences in language and culture among our billions of members of the global body, but in the planetary mind they are all equally of value. And we must remember that beliefs, values, attitudes and other meanings are superimposed out of our need to justify and rationalize giving up the natural state to enter the political state. We superimpose our chosen or conditioned rationality on experience in order to create the illusion that nature is in a static steady state. In fact, dynamic equilibrium and change are the true nature of life. We must be ever prepared to adapt to new conditions in nature with innovative cultural creativity.

Nothing is anything until we make something of it. Life has no inherent meaning. That's the beauty of it. We have developed as organisms to the point where we can make choices on a global scale as to how to live and what to believe. We don't need gods as much as they need us to stay alive.

The Balinese feel that they create the gods, and that in caring for them the gods will in turn care for the people. The unpredictable machinations of both nature and culture cannot be conceived of or dealt with unless individuals are educated and developed to the point at which they can see beyond themselves. That is the end of ignorance and the beginning of understanding.

Then individual and group merge and enter the global identity of the planetary mind that exists in potential in the body of each one of our billions. We are the human beings, and we are the primary beings in support of the planetary mind. We have been here for forty thousand years. What we think of it all is up to us now. There are no gods to turn to, no big guy in the sky, no predictable timepiece cosmos. So, how are we to bring an end to terror?

Security and unity are the same thing. Ideologies, worldviews, and religions and philosophies can best be viewed as notes in a great musical scale. The whole of world religions and philosophies are not exclusive, monolithic and unchanging things. Each point of view is a harmonic interval in the vast concert that is our shared lives. We must not allow immature, undeveloped, and otherwise as yet fully unrealized views to imprison us and take away our freedom as human beings. This leads to a prolongation of conflict, division, separation and alienation. Religions, states, and human beings all experience this sense of being separate as conflict—war, chaos, disorder and unpredictability.

We will be alright when we are all right and realize it. Life is never fair or equitable, neither in nature nor society. But we all own the right to fight or not, to be afraid or not. The end of terror comes when the mind and body realize the nature of unity. All life is engaged in commerce and exchange for the benefit of the development of the greater whole. We can live, for the most part, peacefully while doing so.

Or, we can be afraid and continue to promote war for profit, war for business. We must fear only if we begin to see war as natural. Achieving peace, security and stability is at the root of the effort of the living to develop, to adapt, and to live. When the ability to wage war becomes a nation or individual's power source, the absolute power of destruction corrupts absolutely.

Once globalization completes the course of modernization—natural selection operating on the social and cultural level—we can then humanize our world and decentralize all forms of authority. This is how we bring the end of terror: We become fearless and strong in our identity as world citizens. We expand our self-awareness and become one with, and identical to, the planetary mind.

Suggested Reading

Adler, Alfred. *Understanding Human Nature*. Greenwich: Fawcett Publications, Inc., 1965.

Bateson, Gregory. *Steps Towards an Ecology of Mind*. New York: New American Library, 1972.

Bertalanffy, Ludwig von. *General Systems Theory*. New York: George Braziller, 1968.

Capra, Fritjof. *The Turning Point*. New York: Bantam Books, 1983.

Cressman, L.S. *The Sandal and the Cave: The Indians of Oregon*. Corvallis: OSU Press, 1971.

Carson, Rachel. *Silent Spring*.

Eisler, Riane. *The Chalice and the Blade*. San Francisco: Harper & Row, 1987.

Eisley, Loren. *The Unexpected Universe*.

Freud, Sigmund. *Civilization and its Discontents*.

Geertz, Clifford. *The Interpretation of Cultures*. New York: Basic Books, Inc., 1973.

Gould, Stephen. "Full of Hot Air." *Natural History Magazine* (October, 1989): 38.

Hanneman, Gerhard J. "The Study of Human Communication." *Communication and Behavior*. Reading: Addison-Wesley Publishing Company, 1975.

Hardin, Garrett. *Nature and Man's Fate*. New York: New American Library, 1959.

Harris, Marvin. *Cannibals and Kings: The Origins of Cultures*. New York: Random House, 1977.

Hau de no sau nee. *A Basic Call to Consciousness*. Rooseveltown: Akwesanse Notes, The Mohawk Nation, 1978.

Highwater, Jamake. *The Primal Mind*. New York: New American Library, 1981.

Ishihara, Shintaro. An Untitled Interview. *Time Magazine* (November 20, 1989): 82.

Josephy, Alvin M. *Indian Heritage of America*. New York: Alfred A. Knopf, 1968.

Kraus, James W. *Gary Snyder's Biopoetics, A Study of the Poet As Ecologist*. Unpublished dissertation. Hawaii: Department of American Studies, University of Hawaii.

Kuhn, Thomas S. *The Structure of Scientific Revolutions*. Chicago: The University of Chicago Press, 1970.

Lasch, Christopher. "Beyond Left and Right." *Old Oregon* (Winter, 1989): 21.

Lenneberg, Eric H. *Biological Foundations of Language*. New York: John Wiley & Sons, Inc., 1987.

Leopold, Aldo. *A Sand County Almanac*.

Lovelock & Margulis, *The Gaia Theory*.

Matson, Floyd. *The Broken Image*.

Meadows, Meadows, Randers, & Beherns III. *The Limits to Growth*. New York: New American Library, 1972.

Nakasona, Master. *The Messiah's Return*.

Singer, Marshall. *Intercultural Communications*. New Jersey: Prentice Hall, 1987.

Thomas, Lewis. *The Lives of a Cell: Notes of a Biology Watcher* (& The Medusa and the Snail). New York: Penguin Books, 1985.

Toffler, Alvin. *The Third Wave*. New York: Bantam Books, 1981.

Recommended Periodicals

Discover Magazine
National Geographic
Science Digest
Scientific American

Index

About the Author

MICHAEL W. SIMPSON, PH.D., is a writer of American Indian ancestry from Oregon, who now makes his home in New Mexico.

Dr. Simpson earned a B.G.S. in Written Communications from the University of South Carolina, an M.F.A. in English/Creative Writing from the University of Oregon, and a Ph.D. in American Studies from the University of Hawai'i. He has thirty years of teaching experience at universities in two states and in ten countries around the world.

He has written poetry, essays and novels. He enjoys breeding sphinx cats, restoring cars and dabbling in real estate.

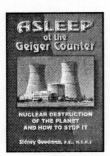

OTHER TITLES
FROM BLUE DOLPHIN PUBLISHING

Improving Relationships
A Guide for Enhancing Personalities Using Nine Personality Types
Albert Heid
ISBN: 1-57733-117-6, 168 pp.,
5x8, paper, $12.95

The Way It Is
One Water, One Air, One Mother Earth
Corbin Harney
ISBN: 0-931892-80-5, 268 pp., 101 photos,
6x9, paper, $16

**People of the Circle,
People of the Four Directions**
Scott McCarthy
ISBN: 1-57733-013-7, paper, 712 pp., 155 illus., 6x9,
paper, $34.95; ISBN: 1-57733-014-5, hardcover, $49.95

Spirit Visions
The Old Ones Speak
Dennison & Teddi Tsosie
ISBN: 1-57733-002-1, 384 pp.,
paper, 6x9, $19.95

Now Is the Hour
Native American Prophecies and Guidance for Earth Changes
Elisabeth Dietz & Shirley Jonas
ISBN: 1-57733-029-3, 112 pp., 5.5 x 8.5, paper, $10

Orders: 1-800-643-0765 • www.bluedolphinpublishing.com

Printed in the United States
25344LVS00004B/187-192

9 781577 331308